What's Cooking
at
MOODY'S
DINER

Library of Congress Control Number: 2003104691
ISBN: 0-89272-631-8
Second Edition

What's Cooking at Moody's Diner: 75 Years of Recipes and Reminiscences

is published by
  Dancing Bear Books
  P.O. Box 4
  West Rockport, Maine 04865

and is exclusively distributed by:
  Down East Books
  P.O. Box 679   Orders: 1-800-685-7962
  Camden, Maine 04843   www.downeastbooks.com

  Down East Books is a division of Down East Enterprise, Inc.,
  publisher of Down East, *the magazine of Maine.*

FIRST PRINTING July 2003

10   9   8   7   6   5   4   3   2   1

Book design: Amy Fischer Design – Camden, Maine
Cover art: Chris Van Dusen – Camden, Maine
Printed in the USA by Versa Press – E. Peoria, Illinois

What's Cooking
at
MOODY'S DINER

75 YEARS OF RECIPES & REMINISCENCES

by
Nancy Moody Genthner

Edited by Kerry Leichtman

Dancing Bear Books
West Rockport, Maine

Distributed by Down East Books

Dedication

Bertha Moody
1902–1977

This cookbook is lovingly dedicated to our mother, Bertha Moody, and contains many of her favorite recipes.

Mom was teaching in a one-room schoolhouse in North Nobleboro, Maine when she met and married Dad. That was in 1922. She was the steady force behind the scenes in Dad's many business ventures, and in each one of our lives.

In the diner's early days, Mom did all the baking at home, either late in the evening or early morning. Summers she managed the cabins; renting units, taking reservations, supervising the cabin girls and cooking a main meal each day for the family and summer help, which meant 12 to 14 people around the table. In the fall, she ran the house and business herself as Dad was away for three months cutting Christmas trees. In the midst of all this Mom raised nine children, and kept a pantry stocked with homemade doughnuts, cookies and other goodies for us to enjoy. It has always amazed me, in thinking about her life, that she did all of this without the benefit of automatic washers and dryers, microwaves, etc., and yet each of us felt loved, special and cared for.

We all have memories of her at the kitchen table after supper helping with homework, packing lunches for school in the morning, frying dozens of doughnuts each week, making birthday cakes, of always being there for us. She was a special lady who will always be remembered with much love and gratitude from each of her children.

Proverbs 31:28: Her children shall rise up and bless her.

Contents

Foreword 6

Greetings, Friends 13

MOODY'S DINER THROUGH THE YEARS, Part I 15

    The History of Moody's Diner 17

    PB Moody 27

    Grammy's Cupboard 35

    The War Effort 41

THE RECIPES

    Diner Recipes 45

    Moody Family Recipes

        Appetizers 63

        Pickles & Relish 65

        Soups 69

        Salads 75

        Breads & Muffins 81

        Main Course Dishes 95

        Casseroles 112

        Vegetables 121

        Desserts 126

        Pies 134

        Cakes 139

        Cookies 148

        Candy & Snacks 165

MOODY'S DINER THROUGH THE YEARS, Part II 169

    Growing Up Moody: Warren's Stories 170

    Moody People 184

    Moody Travelers 192

    A Moody Wedding 202

RECIPE INDEX 203

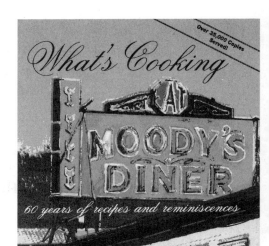

What's Cooking

AT MOODY'S DINER

60 years of recipes and reminiscences

by Nancy Moody Genthner
edited by Kerry Leichtman

Over 35,000 Copies Served!

NEW REVISED EDITION

More:
• Recipes
• Photos
• Stories

What's Cooking at

AT MOODY'S DINER

75 years of Recipes and Reminiscences

by Nancy Moody Genthner
edited by Kerry Leichtman

Foreword

First, you'll want to know what's new in this revised edition of *What's Cooking at Moody's Diner*. We added 59 recipes, deleted 11, and broke down the Moody's Diner recipes into family-sized proportions, saving you the trouble of doing the math. Because many institutional kitchens found the diner-sized quantities useful (there are kids at summer camps across the country dining on Moody's Diner fare), most of the diner recipes are presented in both sizes.

Feedback to the original edition was terrific. Many commented that they found our simple recipes a refreshing contrast to the complex culinary contortions featured in many cookbooks. People also loved the stories and pictures, telling us the reminiscences and Moody family snapshots were as fun to read and look at as the recipes were to use. So in addition to the new recipes we've added loads of new pictures and new stories.

Nancy's brother Alvah, brother-in-law Bill Jones, and sisters Judy Beck and Nellie Jones contributed to the original edition's reminiscences. This time out Nancy cast a wider net. Brothers Warren and Harvey added their memories of growing up Moodys in Waldoboro, Maine, as did the grandchildren of diner founders Bertha and Percy Moody.

Moody family members also contributed recipes. For the original edition, Nancy asked them to send recipes that they associated with Bertha Moody—Mom to Nancy and her siblings, Grandma to their children, and Aunt Bertha to her cousins—which is why many recipes have titles like Aunt Bertha's Casserole, Grandma's Muffins, or Mom's Cookies. The first chapter (pages 45–62) consists of recipes from the diner (most of which originated with Bertha); the others are those collected from the family.

You'll also find, on the recipe pages, a line drawing of a waitress carrying a tray of food. Like most of the waitresses at Moody's, she smiles as she deftly handles an overloaded tray. How fast can she get from the kitchen to your table? That's up to you. Hold the corner of the book under your thumb, flick the pages and watch her move.

And finally, one other thing's new in this revised *What's Cooking*: we're using a new bookbinding method called Otabind. It allows the book to lie open to any page without breaking the binding, which is especially useful when following recipes. It seems to work pretty well, and the closer to the middle, the better. So we—and Nancy insisted on this—divided the stories and photos into two sections and placed them at the book's first and last pages, leaving the middle pages for the recipes. Clever people, those Moody's, always trying to give their customers more value. We hope you find it makes using the book a little easier.

Jeffrey Sprague, great-grandson of Bertha and PB Moody, gives a copy of the recently
published original edition of *What's Cooking at Moody's Diner* to Maine Senator George
Mitchell during a 1990 class trip to Washington D.C. Our Senator Mitchell went on to
become Senate Majority Leader, the book went on to become a regional bestseller, and
Jeffrey is, at this writing, at the University of Maine, Presque Isle, where he's studying to
be a teacher. Jeff took some of the photos in this book.

There are many reasons why Moody's Diner is beloved by so many
people from so many different places. Well, yeah, there's the food, but
there's also something else—an honesty that is becoming increasingly hard
to find. The American Dream is success achieved through hard work and
honesty. Moody's Diner encompasses that ideal.

To illustrate that point, two stories come to mind that are so similar I
can tell them together. In one, a television station from away called to say
they wanted to do a profile on Moody's Diner as part of a series featuring
restaurants across America. Moody's was their choice for Maine. The other
story involves a major women's/home magazine. The television station and
the magazine each wanted to capture the simple country-folk Americana
that is Moody's Diner.

The television people asked Nancy for a New England dish that could be prepared on the air. She sent them some recipes. They responded saying all were too simple; they needed to use up 15 minutes of air time. "But none of our foods take that long to prepare," she told them.

The magazine's food editor called one day and said they wanted to fly a production crew up to Maine the following Monday to photograph the making of New England Boiled Dinner at Moody's Diner. Nancy told them they were welcome to take pictures, but Moody's cooked and served boiled dinner on Thursdays, so come then. "Don't worry," she was told, "and no slight intended to your chef, but we're bringing our own meat and recipe. We just need to use your kitchen Monday morning at 11:00." The editor was probably surprised when Alvah got on the phone and said, if they wanted to photograph the preparation of a Moody's Diner New England Boiled Dinner, they could show up on Thursday—without the groceries.

Those of you who have been to Moody's Diner know that it is not a quaint-on-purpose tourist attraction. It is a diner on U.S. 1 in Waldoboro, Maine, plain and simple. It has survived, prospered and grown these 75 some odd years because of good food, reasonable prices, and quick, pleasant service. There are people who eat at Moody's every day, and those who come in every time they travel to Maine. Both are made welcome. Locals aren't expected to go elsewhere during the tourist season, and tourists aren't gouged for their vacation cash.

Alvah says success came because "it was the only place open 24 hours between Bangor and Portland before they built the interstate, back when Route 1 was the highway." But Alvah was only telling half the story. They work at it—hard. Alvah figured out that if you roast a turkey upside-down, its juices would flow to the breast, making that portion of meat juicier. The pies at Moody's taste fresh because they're baked out back in a separate pastry kitchen by a pastry chef. It would be easier to defrost and sell factory-made pies, but they don't. The crust is always flaky and the meringue tall and perfectly browned, the mashed potatoes come out of skins not a box, and the gravy at Moody's Diner is made from meat drippings rather than poured from jars. I once asked family patriarch PB Moody if he was surprised by how successful Moody's Diner had become. His response was quick: "Of course not. It's run by Moodys."

And it still is. As one generation ages and another takes its place, the constant is the diner itself and the values that sustain it.

So again, whether you're from down the road or across the country, we'll see you next time you stop at Moody's Diner.

Kerry Leichtman
Publisher, Dancing Bear Books

THEN: The author at age 2 with her sister Nellie, in 1937.

NOW: Nancy (right) with another sister, Judy, in 2003.

Greetings, Friends

It has been 14 years since we published our cookbook in June of 1989. Some 50,000 cookbooks later and counting, we are completely amazed and humbled that what started out as a gathering of recipes and stories of the business at the request of some customers has generated such interest.

Since the first edition in 1989, time has brought changes to our family, our business and the world. Our family continues to be a bedrock of love and support as we begin to see the years diminish our numbers. My father, Percy "PB" Moody, the diner's founder, passed away in 1992. The year 2000 brought the loss of my husband, Wayne, and my brother David, who owned Dave's Restaurant in neighboring Thomaston. But "to be absent from the body is to be present with the Lord," and we rejoice in the truth that we will be reunited one day.

In January of 1993, the government released a report detailing the harmful effects of second-hand smoke. The report gave weight to an ongoing concern we had about the diner's "smoking section." We had been shrinking the section for several years, but with our low ceilings and open dining area, the smoke drifted around anyway, and the small smoking section itself became difficult to work in. In May of 1993, as evidence of the hazards of second-hand smoke continued to mount, we decided to become "smoke-free," one of the first restaurants in Maine to take this stand.

In December of 1994, we closed for five weeks for a major renovation, increasing our seating to 104, raising the roof, adding a large pastry kitchen, and increasing the size of our main kitchen. Radiant heat and new air conditioning were installed, as well as new bathrooms. And in March 2000, we took down the "Open 24 Hours" sign and now close at 11:00 P.M. and open at 4:30 in the morning.

In 1998, my husband and I, with my daughter Mary and her husband, established a gift shop across the parking lot from the diner. It has been a great experience, opening us up to the interesting world of retail marketing. The motel is still under the management of my youngest sister, Debbie Bellows, and her husband, Bob. It has been rewarding to serve the next generation of visitors to Maine, and we appreciate those who return each year for a little step back in time to stay at cabins that echo a distant, more simple past in Maine's tourist industry.

As the years have gone by, brothers Harvey, Dewey and Warren, all retired engineers, have built either retirement homes or cottages at Moody's Island in Nobleboro. Judy and her husband, Bob, also a retired engineer, have also built a home at the lake. Our father once operated this large parcel of lakeside property as Moody's Island Campground. When he closed it, he graciously divided the property into cottage lots for his children. It has become a year-round home for three of us and summer vacation spots for the rest. Interest in the family business is shared by all—each spring and summer you will find these retired engineers working together with Alvah and Bill on some new project for the diner or motel. As you will see when you read Warren's boyhood reminiscences, not much has changed there.

Dan Beck, a grandson of PB, has joined the business in management this year. Another grandson, Steve Moody, is a buyer and chef. Great-granddaughters and great-grandsons are dishwashers, line cooks, pastry cooks, cashiers and servers. Some are working to pay for college, others are learning the rewards of that first job. We celebrated our 75th year in business the summer of 2002 and had a photo taken of all the 31 family members currently working in the diner, motel, and gift shop or helping out in maintenance and construction (page 16).

We live in unstable times, but in this little corner of the world we are trying to maintain a family business that has sustained many other families, provided first jobs for hundreds of young people, helped students pay for those ever-rising college costs, and has remained a place you can always come home to, for those from away and those close by. Thanks to all of you who keep coming by and making that possible.

And thanks for purchasing this little cookbook. We hope you enjoy the new photos, the memories of some family members, and the recipes, old and new. I would love to hear from you if you have any questions or comments. You can reach me by regular mail at Moody's Diner, P. O. Box 376, Waldoboro, ME 04572, or by e-mail at info@moodysdiner.com. This being a new millenium, you can also stop by our web site at www.moodys diner.com.

Nancy

MOODY'S DINER
THROUGH THE YEARS

Part I

The History of Moody's Diner
PB Moody • Grammy's Cupboard
The War Effort

Diner founders Bertha and Percy PB Moody

THEN: This picture, taken sometime in the 1940s, features some of the diner's family employees. They are (left to right): Dewey Moody, Nellie Benner, Clara Barton, Virginia Moody, Elsie Winchenbach, Esther Lovette, Thelma Kennedy, Nellie Moody Jones (standing), Austin Achorn (on bicycle).

NOW (below)—In the summer of 2002, three generations of Moodys working the family businesses. They are (back row, left to right) Kim Ward, Ruth Beck, Dan Beck, Sheri Beck, Mary Olson, Nancy Genthner, Alvah Moody, Judy Beck, Nellie Jones, Bill Jones, Jean Moody, Harvey Moody; (2nd row, standing) Rachel Little, Debbie Bellows, Georgetta Moody, Steve Moody; (kneeling) Phillip Bellows, Megan Moody; (front row) Jeff Sprague, Jasmine Olson, Samantha Olson, David Bellows, Jenny Ward, Aaron Beck, Bethany Reed, Leigha Reed, Elizabeth Jones, Nathan Beck, Andrew Beck. Nellie Moody Jones is in both photos. Photo courtesy of *The Lincoln County News*.

The History of Moody's Diner

Mom wrote this history of how the diner got started in 1976. She passed away in 1977. Since then, we expanded the diner once more, now seating 104, and added a gift shop.

In 1927 we built three small cabins. Each had one room and a screened porch with dry toilets up back. There was no running water then; we bought spring water from Mack's Bottle Works in town and took a glass jug of cold water to guests when they came in. The cabins rented for $1.00 per person—that was before the days of sales tax. Since we had no eating place, we sent people downtown to Brown's Restaurant under the old Star Theatre.

Business was good, so the next year we built two two-room cabins and two more one-room cabins. The one-room cabins were fitted out with twin beds. We rented those rooms for $3.00 ($1.50 per person).

The next year, 1929, we drilled a well and built a building for showers and toilets. By 1939 we had our present number of cabins, and all had bathrooms.

During those first years the cabins had no heat, but soon all were equipped with wood stoves. Our sons went around with a wheelbarrow and filled the boxes. Later we installed gas heaters in some of the cabins. Now all have thermostat-controlled electric heat.

In the summer of 1930 we bought a small house by the entrance to the cabins and opened a small restaurant, serving only breakfast and dinner. Next, we installed gasoline pumps in front of the restaurant. The road in front of the cabins and restaurant was Route 1, now it's Route 1A. In either 1931 or '32, we put a very small lunch wagon next to the restaurant and sold hot dogs and hamburgers through the day.

In August 1934 the present Route 1 was opened. We had to buy land there that adjoined ours and then built a road to connect our business with Route 1. We moved the little lunch wagon down to the new Route 1, put a screened porch on the front, and were ready for business when the new road opened. That was where the present Moody's Diner was born. We only served lunch during the first year, and I cooked all the pastry myself at home.

As the business grew we added sections to the little lunch wagon until reaching its present size, with a full basement, a pastry kitchen, seating capacity for 70 and air conditioning. We kept the little restaurant on the hill beside the cabins open for just two summers after the small diner was opened.

by Bertha Moody

I have yet to know of a woman who could make such delicious meals out of leftovers. She was at least as frugal as our father. While cleaning the attic after her death, a box was found, labeled in her handwriting, "String too short to use." That was exactly what it contained. — Harvey Moody

The cabins rented for $1.00 per person. Since we had no eating place, we sent people to Brown's Restaurant. — Bertha Moody

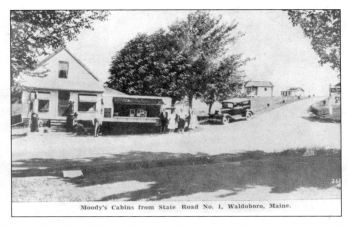

Moody's Cabins from State Road No. 1, Waldoboro, Maine.

The original diner: When it first started, it was just a little stand with an open serving window. Then Dad put a little porch over the front of it. — Alvah Moody

I was 7 years old in 1934, when the road was built from the cabins to the new Route 1. Dad put an ad in the paper for men to work on the road. When we woke up the next morning, the dooryard was full of men, some with horses and some with horses and wagons. A man alone got hired for $1.00 per day, man and horse for $1.50, and a man with horse and wagon for $2.00. A wood-burning steam shovel was used to dig out the bank. Two men worked on it, one operating the shovel and one stoking the fire. The steam came out of the boom. Dad let us sit up in the woods to watch. It sure made a lot of noise. — Alvah Moody

MOODY'S CABINS
WALDOBORO, ME.

When Dad moved it down to the new Route 1, he went over the whole thing
and wound up with a door at each end. — Alvah Moody

Among this day's lunch crowd was the Moxie HorseMobile (on the right), a horse
model mounted on a car chassis that was used for parades, fairs and other promotions by
the Moxie Company. Moxie, originating in Union, Maine, was first marketed as patent
medicine, a cure-all for a wide variety of ills—from "loss of manhood" to "softening of the
brain." It was later marketed as a beverage that, until dethroned by Coca-Cola in the
1920s, was the nation's most popular soft drink. It's still being sold today.

Next, he added on to the back of the diner, and put in the ladies' and men's rooms.
Then he built a piece for a woodshed. The next year he continued the end where
the horseshoe counter is now and made a dining room. — Alvah Moody

Above: In 1948, Dad put a dining room on the other end and moved the door to the front. Then, in 1949, we moved the back wall of the kitchen out five feet. It was the same year I built my house. I took the crew over on a Saturday night and we cut the wall right out, put it on some pipes and rolled it right out. We studded up the roof, left the fans on the wall and had an electrician extend the wiring, and started cooking in the new space the next morning. It seemed like we had all kinds of room. Bill Jones said I'd get lost with all that new space. — Alvah Moody

Photo by Jeff Sprague

Moody's Diner, 2003. The last time the diner's outside appearance changed was in 1994. The original counter is still in the center, up to the cash register. — Alvah Moody

Alvah Moody and Bill Jones in their domain. Alvah and Bill ran the kitchen for 50+ years, with time off to serve their country. Moody's was established the year Alvah was born. He began working as a dishwasher there at age 12. Bill met Nellie while serving in the Navy and worked in the diner until retiring a few years ago.

When Eben and Jim came to Moody's for the photo shoot of their "now" picture on the facing page, Eben said he was as old as the diner. "So's Alvah," we told him, and then called Alvah into the dining room. The two got to talking, and as it turned out, their birthdays are just four days apart, Alvah being the youngster.

THEN: Everyone's favorite photo from the first edition of *What's Cooking at Moody's Diner* was taken by Patrick Downs in 1984.

NOW: Eben Sawyer and his grandson, Jim Pendergast, Jr., nineteen years later.

In March 1998, we upgraded to a brand-new neon sign—same design but (hopefully) with more reliable electronics. Below, the old sign is getting a send-off from (left to right) Alvah, Nancy and Warren after being loaded into a trailer pulled by a beautifully restored 1967 International Travelall. Its new owner, neon collector Dave Waller of Malden, Massachusetts, lent the sign to diner historian Richard Gutman, who is curating, "Diners in the 21st Century," an exhibit at Johnson & Wales' Culinary Archives & Museum in Providence, Rhode Island. The exhibit will continue into 2008.

Photo by Dave Waller

THEN: Glenda and Mary Sukeforth, Laura Leonard, Avis Luce, Del Overlock
and Pat Lailor, sometime in the 1950s.

NOW: Waitresses left to right: Kathie Hills, Pam Thibodeau, Tami Lee,
Kathy Kinney and Dianne Burnham.

An interviewer once asked Dad if
he had any ideas on how to make a
million dollars. "No," he replied,
"but I have a million ideas on how
to make a dollar."

Few people know the extent of our father's enterprises. In addition to the diner and cabins,
there was a working farm with 15 to 20 milking cows, 20 pigs, a horse, laying hens and
200+ acres of land; a Christmas tree business that shipped 5,000 trees to Boston; a light
construction company; and, for a short while, a lakeside campground. — Harvey Moody

PB Moody

Most people knew Dad as "PB." He was born in 1900 in North Nobleboro, the youngest of seven children. He attended high school at Lincoln Academy, traveling by horse and buggy to the train station, and from there to the academy in Damariscotta. His parents took in summer boarders for vacations at their home on Damariscotta Lake, so he fell in quite naturally to the tourist business.

Dad moved to Waldoboro when he and Mom married in 1922. He seemed to have boundless energy and thrived on hard work. He'd catnap in his Morris chair for fifteen minutes and then jump up refreshed to tackle another job. In the early years, he did many things to earn a living; peddling fish door to door, smelting, raising vegetables for a roadside stand, to mention a few.

When he started the diner, he kept a large vegetable garden, raised beef steers and pigs, hayed, and kept dairy animals for both the family and the business. In the fall he'd leave home for three months to continue his father's Christmas tree business. He would come home every Saturday night and leave again Sunday night for upstate. In his absence, Mom would care for all of us children, oversee the diner and handle telephone orders for Christmas trees.

Each year, Dad shipped five or six carloads of Christmas trees (totaling about 5,000 trees) by rail to the old Charlestown freight yard in Boston. Mom would travel to Boston with him for two weeks in early December to sell the trees. They stayed at a rooming house on Mass. Avenue with Dad going off to the freight yard in the morning and Mom going by subway into Boston to do her Christmas shopping. I have often thought what a vacation that must have been for her, to be relieved of caring for all of us and to think only of herself and Dad, and best of all to eat all her meals out!

It was with great excitement that we would watch for them to arrive home from Boston. They would drive in, the car loaded with the results of Mom's shopping. Dad would smell of fir. We'd watch with anticipation as the car was unpacked. The smell of fir today ushers in memories of those exciting days before Christmas.

In December 1954, while I was attending college in Providence, Rhode Island, I went by train to Boston and spent a weekend with my parents during their annual two weeks there. It was a great experience to see my parents in these unusual surroundings. I have never forgotten it.

Dad was not one who cared for possessions. He rarely spent money on himself, didn't drive new expensive cars (loved his Chevys), in fact even the farm equipment was old and continually repaired—he came from the generation of "making do." But he was the consummate entrepreneur, always on the alert for new ideas. He was once asked by an interviewer if he had any ideas on how to make a million dollars. His reply was, "No, but I have a million ideas on how to make a dollar."

His generosity of spirit was brought home to us after his death when we received a letter from a neighbor down the hill from Dad's home. She wanted to let the family know her appreciation for Dad. When her well had gone dry during a rain-free summer, he ran a line down from the water supply of the cabins and provided her with water for as long as she needed and would accept no payment. These stories were repeated in various ways many times and were a testament to a man who naturally extended a helping hand and wanted no publicity for himself.

My brother Harvey has a similar recollection: "Years after my father's death I still hear stories from people my father helped. Many I never knew about, and I suspect most people never did either. When I was in elementary school, the town and school were in the process of building a baseball field beyond the high school. I spent many hours with my father and the hired help cutting brush, grading and raking the field, putting up fences and building bleachers. It didn't stop there; he also ran the concession stand, selling hot-dogs, pop, and candy bars, with the proceeds going to the local twilight league team. As much as I wanted to watch the games, I was expected to help with the sales and clean up afterward. But it wasn't all work. One time we were burning brush at the ball field. Dad took one look at the resulting bed of glowing coals and went for hot dogs, rolls and pop. We sat around the fire in the gathering darkness cooking and eating hot dogs."

He was a firm father. We were expected to obey his rules and be ready to work wherever or whatever, to be courteous and respectful. We all chafed a little under that discipline, but it has served us well in life. At the same time, if he ever became aware of needs in our life that he could provide, he was there with some cash or his crew to help out. College or the establishment of a career was his goal for us. We were expected to embrace his aspiration for us by working summers to provide some of our own means to achieve our goals. The nine of us became three engineers, two nurses, two medical secretaries and two restaurant owners.

As children, we sometimes complained about his firmness, but in later days appreciated his example of hard work and determination. We all truly believe the happiness and success of our lives is strongly tied to the love and discipline of two very special people—our parents.

We often get inquiries from Moodys researching family roots. Harvey is our family historian and has kindly provided the genealogy of the PB Moody family on p. 30. We hope this will be helpful for all genealogy buffs.

Dad's family came from North Nobleboro, Maine. Here the family is gathered at the old Moody farm. Pictured are Dad's grandparents, Hannah and Joshua Moody (seated in the middle), his parents, Emma and Asa (standing 4th and 5th from the left), and his uncles and their wives. Two of Dad's uncles heeded Horace Greeley's call to "Go west, young man," ending up in Oregon and California.

PB Moody Family GENEALOGY

Edmund Moody   (1495– ?)   Bury St. Edmunds, Suffolk, England.
                                Granted a coat of arms in 1540 for
                                saving the life of King Henry VIII.

Richard Moody (1525–1574)   Moulton, Suffolk, England

Robert Moody   (1563– ?)   Robert's brother George is an ancestor
                                of Dwight L. Moody, founder of Moody
                                Institute.

William Moody (1580– ?)   Sudbury, Suffolk, England

William Moody (1611–1673)   Ipswich, Suffolk, England. Saddler by
                                trade. Came to Ipswich, Massachusetts,
                                in 1634 on ship *Mary & John.*

Caleb Moody   (1637–1698)   Lived and built a home in
                                Newburyport, Massachusetts.

Daniel Moody I (1622–1717)   Resided in Newbury and Salisbury,
                                Massachusetts.

Daniel Moody II (1684–1760)   Resided in Salisbury, Massachusetts,
                                Stratham, New Hampshire,
                                and Scarborough, Maine

John Moody   (1718–1778)   Born in Stratham, New Hampshire.
(also known   Resided in Scarborough, Maine, in
as Joshua)   1724 and Nobleboro, Maine, in 1758.

Amos Moody, Sr. (1747–1847)   Resided in North Nobleboro, Maine.

Daniel Moody   (1778–1854)   Resided in North Nobleboro, Maine
                                and moved to Liberty, Maine in 1844.

Joshua Moody   (1796–1887)   Resided in North Nobleboro, Maine.

Joshua B. Moody (1821–1903)   Resided in North Nobleboro, Maine.

Asa I. Moody   (1859–1933)   Resided North Nobleboro and
                                Waldoboro, Maine.

Percy B. Moody (1900–1992)   Resided North Nobleboro and
                                Waldoboro, Maine.

This genealogy was developed using ancestry charts from the Moody Bible Institute, from Dr. David L. Moody of St. Paul, Minnesota, from *Four Generations of the descendents of William Moody of Newbury, Massachusetts, in 1635,* by Noreen C. Pramburg, from the research of Harold Moody of Exeter, N.H., and from the vital records of Nobleboro and Bristol, Maine.

The name Moody is of English origin and was a term of endearment or nickname given to those who distinguished themselves in battle. Many with the Moody surname are not related by blood but by the actions of their ancestors, which makes the development of ancestral charts especially challenging.

Edmund Moody saved King Henry the VIII of England from drowning in a hunting accident. For this he was granted a coat of arms and given an estate. William Moody, the great-great-grandson of Edmund, came to Massachusetts in 1634, settling in Newburyport. He is known to have had at least three sons: Samuel, Joshua and Caleb. His home, as well as that of his son Caleb, is still standing to date. A large portion of the Moodys in northern New England can be traced to them.

My Uncle Lloyd relates the stories told him of his great-great-great-great-grandfather John Moody's move from Scarborough, Maine, to Nobleboro. They came in two oxen-drawn wagons with their farm animals alongside. They lived in one of the wagons and carried their household goods in the other. A trip that now takes us two hours by car took them two months.

Harvey Moody

Dad was one of seven children: four boys and three girls. This photo shows him with brothers Lloyd, Irving and Louis. PB, the youngest, is in the front. Louis died during the influenza epidemic in 1918.

The Moody family, 1942

The Moody family, 1952

Below: The Moody siblings in 1992, in the same positions as in the above 1952 photo.
They are (back, left to right): Nellie, David, Warren, Alvah, Dewey, Nancy;
(seated, left to right) Harvey, Debbie, Judy.

THEN: Great-granddaughters Bethany Reed and Jasmine Olson.

NOW: Bethany and Jasmine, 2003.

Grammy's Cupboard

Grandparents are an important part of a family, which is what God intended them to be. My mom was one of those special Grammies to all of her 26 grandchildren. She was the family's super glue, and all counted it a great privilege to go to Grammy's house. Each was always met with a big hug; she was available to read books and play games, and she kept a pantry full of goodies. When she knew someone was going to visit, her kitchen came alive and the aroma of chocolate chip and molasses cookies filled the house. She did not have a toy chest, but a toy closet filled with the same toys we had all enjoyed while growing up. What a treat for the children to open the closet door and haul out all its treasures onto the living room floor. These sturdy wooden toys, worn dolls, metal tea sets, Tinkertoys and metal toy soldiers would entertain for hours yet another generation.

We planned on creating a section called Grammy's Cupboard in our new gift shop to display kitchen and food products, dedicating the space to Mom. Granddaughter Christine Beck Reed used the letters from the title, Grammy's Cupboard, to give form to her fond memories. We wound up using the space differently, but I'm pleased to present Christine's remembrances to you here:

G — God's gift to her grandchildren
R — Reason to go home to Maine
A — Amazing
M — Meekness
M — Memories for a lifetime
Y — Yummy molasses cookies
S — Saturday morning doughnuts

C — Closet full of toys
U — Unbelievably soft skin
P — Patient
B — Biscuits (Michael thanks you)
O — Over-flowing house at Christmas
A — Available anytime
R — Ready for double, triple or quadruple solitaire
D — Dimes for the soda machine in the office

Some of Mom and Dad's other grandchildren also contributed memories for the collection of reminiscences on the following pages.

PB and Bertha celebrate their 50th wedding anniversary.

The Long Trip to Grammy's House

Traveling to Grammy's up in Maine was a trip that lasted an eternity, or at least it seemed that way to a little boy from Connecticut. The first four hours were almost bearable, but that last hour from Brunswick to Waldoboro along the "scenic" Route 1 was enough to put this restless tyke over the edge. The final stretch of the trip, with a snoring brother on one side and a sister slumped into my piece of back seat on the other, never seemed to come to an end. All this while the hot summer air roared through the open windows, as my Dad, in my opinion, could not go fast enough down the endless Route 1.

Cramped, tired and restless, I would watch in desperation for the one landmark that promised light at the end of the tunnel—the Moody's Diner sign, high among the pines on the right-hand side of northbound Route 1. We'd cross the top of the hill and, descending into the Waldoboro valley, I could see the Texaco station on the left and knew relief was only minutes away. Grammy's house was near! Hallelujah!!!

Route 1 did have an end! For this little boy, it ended in Grammy and

Grandpa's driveway. As we climbed out of the car and walked into the house, the delicious smell of molasses cookies would greet our noses. And then came that moment, the moment that made the misery of the eternal trip disappear, Grammy's hug. Her skin was so soft, her hug so gentle, and her perfume so sweet and memorable. (My Mom says she wore L'Origan; I still can pick out that scent anywhere.) Grammy was a special treasure who made our journeys to Maine worth every last "eternal Route 1" second.

Dan Beck

Being One of PB's Grandkids

My very earliest memories of Grampa are of him coming to our house in the morning each day to get the menus. Sometimes Mom wouldn't have them done, and we would rush to grab some books and sit on Grampa's lap so he could read to us while he waited. I can still hear his voice, the way he cleared his throat and the way he smelled. It's funny how a few years later we still rushed around when Grampa came for the menus, but it was to rush upstairs because it was 10:30 Saturday morning and we weren't dressed yet!

Memories of Christmas at Grammy and Grampa's are my most cherished. A Christmas doesn't come and go that I don't stop for a minute and see my grandparents sitting side by side in the living room surrounded by heaps of presents, kids and wrapping paper. Those were wonderful times that I know we all treasure.

There was something about Grampa that made you want to go the extra mile, he always expected the best. We would sure snap to attention when he would arrive at the diner, no overcrowding dishes in the dishwasher or giving too much butter with the biscuits. Once Grampa called an old boyfriend of mine a "good-looking chap." I'm sure he didn't realize how much that meant to me; if Grampa thought something was good, then it must be good indeed!

I think back to the first time I realized that Grampa was somewhat famous in the community. I was in the 4th grade, and someone in my class said, "PB Moody is *your* grandfather!"

I sure gained status that day. I know that has happened to all of us grandchildren at some point, especially to those of us who have lived or been away from Waldoboro. The diner and Grampa's name comes up in job interviews, on airplanes, and with anyone who asks where we are from. Grampa left us a rich heritage of memories that we can be very proud of. He was truly a legend in his own time.

Anne Braley

Grammy could heal your hurts with one of her sweet smiles, soft hugs, or an ever-present cookie. She made the simple things in life special to a young girl, often with just a coin for a soda out of the old machine in the office. Grammy set an example of what a lady, a wife, a mother and grandmother should be like. She didn't preach or scold, just lovingly taught all those around her how to live life.

Pat Jones Caldwell

I can still picture the food closet filled with lemon cakes, donuts, molasses cookies and bags of candy to fill the candy dishes for Grandpa. I can't forget the toy closet filled with the Hula Hoops, Uncle Wiggily board game, the doll furniture I loved playing with, and much more.

Mary Genthner Olson

Grammy had a gold charm bracelet that she wore often which contained a charm for each of her grandchildren. Each charm was in the shape of either a girl or boy's head with the name and birthdate of a grandchild engraved on it. Whenever she moved, the bracelet made a jingling sound that I still remember. We had fun searching for our own charm whenever she wore it.

Cathy Genthner Hopler

Christmas Day contains special memories of afternoons spent at Grammy and Grampa's with our cousins, aunts and uncles. After a huge turkey dinner with all the fixin's, Grammy and Grampa would sit in their favorite living room chairs with presents piled around them in tall stacks. They would open each one slowly and remark how lovely it was. It was a chance for all of us to give a little back to two people who had given us so much in so many ways.

Cathy Genthner Hopler

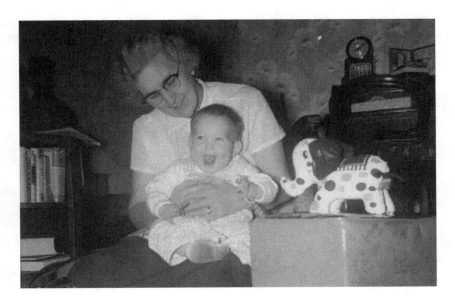

Grandson Dan Beck manages the diner now.

Grandson Steve Moody is a buyer and cook.

The War Effort

My sister Nellie vividly recalled a day when Dad shut the diner down to feed a troop convoy that was traveling south from the Limestone airbase on their way to deployment in Europe during WWII.

"When the servicemen came down from Limestone that day, we closed the diner there were so many—a great big convoy of them. It was the middle of the afternoon in the winter. Oh, it was cold—there was snow and wind blowing. They were in open command cars. The back was closed, but only with canvas, and where the men drove it was completely open. They all had facemasks on.

"Dad closed the diner and Clara came up and we made more doughnuts and we laid everything out and they came in one door and went out the other, a line of them picking up food as they walked through."

Nellie, in her diner uniform, framed by the door through which the soldiers entered.

Bill Jones met Nellie while
serving in the Navy.

Moody's Diner Assists Santa For Third Year

Although Santa Claus gets busy only once a year the staff at Moody's Diner make their Christmas giving a year around affair. For the past three years the entire staff has seen that every local boy received a remembrance from the Diner where they used to drop in so frequently.

The first year the staff chipped in and made delicious home-made fruitcakes and the Christmas package contained cigarettes and fruitcake, sent to servicemen.

Last year the ingredients for fruitcakes wre lacking so that home-made candy and cigarettes went out to all corners of the globe.

This year it will again be fruitcakes and cigarettes and every local boy has been remembered, although doubtful addresses may receive only a card -- at least the staff at Moody's has remembered them all. In talking with P. B. Moody who professed to know "little about it" and "have little to do with it", "They handle it all themselves and any boy local or otherwise who has an address on file will be remembered".

The waitresses, chefs, the pastry cook, and the dishwashers all contribute a portion of their paychecks each week throughout the year so that they may have a fund sufficient to remember all the boys in blue and khaki. The addresses are sought with painstaking care, and each package carefully wrapped and addressed.

The entire project is voluntary on the part of the staff. Mrs. Nellie Benner acts as a co-ordinator for the project. Hats off to these busy people who still have time and inclination to make this friendly gesture!

Whether it was for the local baseball teams or the home boys serving in the armed forces, PB Moody, his family, and staff were always eager to help the community, as this article illustrates. Reprinted courtesy of the *Lincoln County News*.

Alvah in his Navy uniform.

Alvah and Bill on Wartime Waldoboro:

Alvah: During the 1940s they had patrols all the time, day and night, all along the coast.

Before I went into the Navy I used to go up to the station at night. We were supposed to watch for airplanes. I was 15 or 16 years old at the time. Windows were all covered with black gauze so the lights wouldn't shine outside. The civil defense groups all wore black clothes in the streets. They had flashlights that were almost all covered so they only made a small spot of light on the ground.

The Army used to check to make sure civil defense people were at their posts. They went all over.

Bill: Everyone took it seriously. They thought the Germans would land submarines here on the coast.

MOODY'S DINER
LUNCH   MENU

-—HOT DRINKS—-
Chocolate ...... Coffee ...... Tea
Malted Milk ...... Postum

-—SANDWICHES—-
ALL TOASTED SANDWICHES 5C EXTRA

Ham .. 10c   Ham & Eggs .. 20c
Bacon .. 10c Bacon & Egg .. 20c
Cheese .. 10c   Fried Egg .. 10c
Hamburg, steamed rolls 10c
Eastern .. 20c   Western .. 20c
35¢ Chicken 25c Cream Cheese 10c
Cream Cheese & Nut 15c
Cream Cheese & Olive 15c
Cream Cheese & Date 15c
Peanut Butter 10c
~~Lobster .. 20c~~ Crabmeat .. 20c *35¢*
Ham & Cheese 15c
Salmon Salad .... ~~15c~~ *20¢*
Bread & Butter 5c
Chopped Ham, mayonnaise ~~10c~~ *15¢*
We serve hot meat sandwiches
Any Combination Sandwich
will be made on request.
Sandwiches to take out
(over)

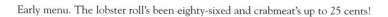

Early menu. The lobster roll's been eighty-sixed and crabmeat's up to 25 cents!

 Diner Recipes

The recipes in this section are of the quantity made at the diner. I have down-sized many of them for family-size meals.

Moody's Fish Chowder

25 lbs. haddock fillets
10 quarts potatoes, diced
8 cups onion, chopped
12 (12 oz.) cans evaporated milk

$1^1/2$ pints all-purpose cream
$^1/2$ lb. margarine
salt and pepper

Place fish in large kettle; cover with water and cook until fish flakes apart. Remove fish. Add potatoes and onions to stock (if necessary add more water to cover potatoes) and cook until potatoes are tender. Add milk, cream, margarine, salt and pepper. Add cooked, flaked fish. Let stand 1 hour to blend flavors. Makes 20 to 24 servings.

This was our original recipe, we now use a steamer to cook this. The following version is in smaller, family-sized proportions and uses a commercial steamer.

Commercial Steamer Recipe:

4 lbs. haddock
2 cups onions, diced
3 quarts potatoes, diced
3 (12 oz.) cans evaporated milk

2 pints half and half
$^1/2$ lb. margarine
salt and pepper

Steam fish and onions for 15 minutes and remove. Steam potatoes for 15 minutes. Heat evaporated milk, half and half and margarine until hot (do not boil). Combine with fish, onions and potatoes and let stand to blend flavors. Add salt and pepper to flavor. Makes 10 to 12 servings.

Clam Chowder Variation:

Same instructions and ingredients as above, only replace haddock with $^1/2$ gallon clam strips. Add 1 Tbsp clam base to milk mixture (optional).

Family-Size Fish Chowder:

1/4 cup margarine
2/3 cup onions, diced
3 cups potatoes, diced
2 lbs. haddock

2 cups milk
1 can evaporated milk
salt and pepper

Melt 2 Tbsp margarine in kettle over medium heat, sauté onions until tender. Add potatoes, cover with water, and place fish on top of potatoes. Cover pot and simmer 20 minutes. Stir in scalded milk and remaining margarine. Season with salt and pepper. Let stand 30 minutes to enhance flavor. Serves 6.

Vegetable Beef Stew

6 lbs. stew beef
1 cup Worcestershire sauce
5 lbs. potatoes, peeled and diced
4 cups celery, chopped
18 carrots, sliced
2 Tbsp beef bouillon powder

3 cups frozen peas
4 cups onions, diced
parsley flakes
1 #10 can stewed tomatoes
3 bay leaves
salt and pepper

Sauté beef in Worcestershire sauce. Add water to cover and cook until tender. Remove meat from pot. Add potatoes, celery and carrots, beef bouillon and enough water to cover vegetables. Cook 30 to 35 minutes. Add frozen peas last 10 minutes. Add meat and parsley flakes. (Thicken, if desired, with a roux of 1 1/2 lbs margarine and flour. Melt margarine in saucepan, add enough flour to make a smooth paste. Add to stew and bring just to a boil to thicken.) Add any other leftover vegetables you like. Makes 20 to 24 servings.

Family-Size Vegetable Beef Stew:

1 lb. stew beef
2 Tbsp Worcestershire sauce
3 beef bouillon cubes
6 med. potatoes, diced
1/2 cup celery, chopped

6 med. carrots, sliced
1/2 cup frozen peas
1 bay leaf
parsley flakes
1 (14 oz.) can stewed tomatoes

Sauté beef in Worcestershire sauce. Add water to cover and cook until tender. Remove meat from pot. Add bouillon cubes to pot and dissolve. Add potatoes, celery, carrots and tomatoes; add enough water to cover vegetables. Cook 30 minutes, add peas last 10 minutes. Add meat and parsley flakes. Serves 6.

Pea Soup

2 gallons water
7 (1 lb.) pkgs. dried peas
4 cups onions, chopped

4 cups ham, cut in bite-sized pieces
salt and pepper

Soak peas and chopped onions in water overnight. Put peas in large kettle, add water and simmer on low heat 1½ hours. Stir often while cooking. Add ham last 15 minutes of cooking. Salt and pepper to taste. Serve with Johnny Cake. Makes 20 servings.

Johnny Cake

6 cups flour
3 Tbsp baking powder
3 cups cornmeal
1 tsp salt

2 cups sugar
4 eggs
1½ cups oil
5 cups milk

Sift dry ingredients. Beat eggs and add to dry ingredients. Mix well, then add oil. Mix and add milk. Stir and pour batter into greased 12 x 18 inch pan and bake 1 hour at 350°. Makes 24 servings.

New England Boiled Dinner

10 lb. corned bottom round
   (with spice pack)
30 whole peeled potatoes

30 whole peeled carrots
30 slices turnip
30 slices cabbage

Place corned round and spices in pressure cooker and cook 35 minutes at 15 lbs. Remove meat to steam table. Put vegetables in pressure cooker and cook 15 minutes at 15 lbs. Place vegetables in steam table. Slice corned beef and serve with potato, carrot, cabbage and turnip. Accompany with vinegar and mustard and a side of buttered beets.

Red Flannel Hash

We used to have this at home with leftovers from boiled dinner—however we don't have it at the diner, as we never have any leftover boiled dinner!

Chop meat and any vegetables. Put in a skillet with some bacon drippings or melted margarine. Heat through and serve. Can also be made with canned corned beef, chopped onions, diced cooked potatoes. Adding chopped beets makes the hash red.

Moody's Meatloaf

Original Recipe:

10 lbs. ground beef
3 cups chopped onion
$^{1}/_{2}$ lb. crushed saltines
10 eggs

$1^{1}/_{2}$ quarts milk
salt and pepper
4 (10 oz.) cans tomato soup

Combine ground beef, onions and saltines. Stir in eggs, milk and seasoning. Divide meat into 4 large loaf pans. Bake 45 minutes at 350°. Remove from oven and pour tomato soup over meatloaf. Return to oven and bake 45 minutes longer. Makes 40 servings.

New Recipe:

10 lbs. ground beef
2 cups onion, chopped
$^{1}/_{2}$ lb. box of saltines, crushed
4 cups oatmeal
7 eggs

4 cups milk
$^{1}/_{4}$ cup French onion soup mix
2 (10 oz.) cans tomato soup
$^{1}/_{4}$ cup Worcestershire sauce
catsup

Combine ground beef, onions, saltines and oatmeal. Stir in eggs, milk, onion soup mix, tomato soup and Worcestershire sauce. Put in 12 x 6 baking pans. Bake at 350° for $1^{1}/_{2}$ hours. Cover top of loaves with catsup for last 5 minutes of baking. Makes 3 pans.

Family-size recipes for meatloaf found on pages 106–107.

Homemade Vegetable Soup

2 quarts chicken stock
1 gallon potatoes, diced
$^{3}/_{4}$ gallon celery, diced
$^{3}/_{4}$ gallon onions, diced
$^{3}/_{4}$ gallon carrots, sliced
1 ($2^{1}/_{2}$ lbs.) bag frozen peas
1 ($2^{1}/_{2}$ lbs.) bag frozen corn

1 (#10) can stewed, chopped
   tomatoes
2 cups catsup
1 Tbsp Bell's seasoning
3 Tbsp chopped garlic
1 Tbsp oregano
salt and pepper

Put chicken stock in large pot, add potatoes, celery, onions, carrots, peas, corn and stewed tomatoes. Cook until vegetables are done, about 20 to 25 minutes. Add catsup, Bell's seasoning, garlic, oregano and salt and pepper. Cook 5 minutes more. Makes 20 quarts.

Homemade Turkey Rice Soup

1 bunch celery, sliced
3 medium onions, chopped
1 tsp minced garlic
$^1/_4$ cup margarine
2 gallons of turkey, or chicken stock
8 cups carrots, sliced

2 cups rice
3 cups turkey, cooked and chopped
1 (50 oz.) can tomato soup
2 cups cabbage, shredded
1 tsp Bell's seasoning

Sauté celery, onions, and garlic in margarine in large kettle. Add chicken stock and heat to boiling. Add carrots and rice and cook 15 minutes. Add tomato soup, shredded cabbage and Bell's seasoning. Cook 10 minutes more. Makes 24 servings.

Moody's Three-Bean Salad

1 (14 to 16 oz.) can green beans
1 (14 to 16 oz.) can yellow beans
1 (14 to 16 oz.) can kidney beans
$^1/_2$ cup onion, chopped
$^1/_2$ cup celery, chopped

$^3/_4$ cup vinegar
$^1/_4$ cup oil
$^1/_4$ tsp pepper
$^1/_2$ cup sugar
$^1/_4$ cup water

Drain and rinse all the beans. Mix beans together with onion and celery. For dressing, combine vinegar, oil, pepper, sugar, and water. Pour over salad. Refrigerate several hours or overnight. Makes 24 servings.

Moody's Mincemeat

3 cups cooked ground beef
9 cups ground apples
1 lb. ground raisins
1 lb. whole seedless raisins
$^3/_4$ lb. margarine
5 cups sugar
1 tsp allspice

$2^1/_2$ cups hot coffee
$^1/_2$ cup vinegar
1 tsp salt
2 tsp cloves
2 tsp cinnamon
2 tsp nutmeg

Combine all ingredients in large kettle and cook over moderate heat. Stir often, as mincemeat will easily burn on. Cook approximately one hour or until mixture darkens. Seal in jars while hot. Makes 7 to 8 pints.

Alvah makes 90 quarts of this recipe each fall so we can serve warm mince-meat pie at the diner in November and December.

DAILY HOMEMADE DESSERT SPECIALS

Moody's Apple Cobbler

6 cups flour
1 tsp salt
1 cup sugar
3 Tbsp baking powder
2 Tbsp cinnamon

4 eggs
3 cups milk
1 cup vegetable oil
10 to 12 cups sliced apples

Topping:

1 cup sugar

1 Tbsp cinnamon

Sift together flour, salt, sugar, cinnamon and baking powder. Beat eggs, add milk and beat again. Pour eggs and milk into dry ingredients, add oil and stir well. Cut up 2 cups of sliced apples and stir into batter. Pour into greased 12 x 18 inch pan and arrange remaining sliced apples over top, pressing lightly into batter. Sprinkle with topping mixture. Bake 30 to 40 minutes at 350°.

Serve warm, topped with the following sauce. Makes 24 servings.

Sauce:

1 lb. margarine
6 cups water
4 cups sugar

$^3/_4$ cup cornstarch
2 tsp vanilla or lemon flavoring

Melt margarine in water in large saucepan. Combine sugar and cornstarch in small bowl. Add approximately 2 Tbsp cool water and blend into a smooth paste. Stir into hot water in saucepan and bring to a boil. Cook a few minutes until thickened. Remove from heat and add flavoring. Serve over hot apple cobbler.

Apple Crisp

14 to 16 cups apples, sliced
2 cups oatmeal
2 cups brown sugar

$2^1/_4$ cups flour
1 Tbsp cinnamon
$^3/_4$ lb. margarine

Line a greased 12 x 18 inch pan with $^3/_4$-inch layer of sliced apples. Combine oatmeal, brown sugar, flour and cinnamon in large bowl. Cut in margarine until mixture resembles coarse crumbs and sprinkle over apples. Bake 35 to 40 minutes at 350°. Serve warm with whipped cream. Serves 24.

Family-Size Apple Crisp:

$^1/_2$ cup oatmeal	$^3/_4$ tsp cinnamon
$^2/_3$ cup brown sugar	$^1/_3$ cup margarine
$^1/_2$ cup flour	4 cups sliced apples

Use 8-inch-square pan and follow directions above.

Bread Pudding

14 eggs	$^1/_2$ tsp salt
6 quarts milk	3 tsp vanilla
1 cup sugar	40 slices of bread, cut in
1 Tbsp nutmeg	small pieces
1 Tbsp cinnamon	$^1/_2$ lb. raisins

Beat eggs; add milk and sugar and mix well. Stir in spices and vanilla. Place bread in 12 x 18 inch pan. Pour egg and milk mixture over bread and stir. Stir in raisins. Bake 2$^1/_2$ hours at 350°, stirring occasionally. Serves 24.

Family-Size Bread Pudding:

3 cups soft bread crumbs	$^1/_4$ tsp salt
2 cups milk, scalded	1 tsp cinnamon, or nutmeg
$^1/_4$ cup margarine	1 tsp vanilla
$^1/_3$ cup sugar	$^1/_2$ cup raisins
2 eggs, slightly beaten	

Place crumbs in 1$^1/_2$ qt. baking dish. Blend in 2 cups scalded milk with $^1/_4$ cup margarine, sugar, slightly beaten eggs, salt, spices and vanilla. Stir in raisins. Bake at 350° for 40 minutes, stirring occasionally.

Grape-Nut Custard Pudding

12 eggs	1 tsp vanilla
3 cups sugar	1 tsp salt
3 quarts milk	2^1/$_4$ cups Grape-Nuts cereal

Beat eggs; add sugar, salt, vanilla and grapenuts and mix well. Stir in milk. Pour into 12 x 18 inch pan and bake 1 hour at 350°. Serves 24.

Family-Size Grape-Nut Custard:

4 eggs	^{1}/$_2$ tsp vanilla
1 cup sugar	^{1}/$_4$ tsp salt
^{3}/$_4$ cup Grape-Nuts cereal	1 quart milk

Follow directions above, use 9 x 13 pan.

Grape-Nut Pudding

1 gallon milk	10 Tbsp flour
1 (16 oz.) box Grape-Nuts cereal	8 eggs, separated
2 cups sugar	^{1}/$_4$ cup sugar

In top of double boiler, combine and heat milk and grapenuts. In large bowl, mix together 2 cups sugar, egg yolks and flour. Add a little milk to make a smooth paste, then add to warm milk in double boiler. Cook until thickened. In separate bowl, beat egg whites. When eggs are fluffy, add ^{1}/$_4$ cup sugar and beat until egg whites are stiff. Fold egg whites into cooked pudding. Serve topped with whipped cream. Serves 20.

Family-Size Grape-Nut Pudding:

1 quart milk	2^1/$_2$ Tbsp flour
^{1}/$_2$ cup sugar	2 eggs, separated
1 cup Grape-Nuts cereal	2 Tbsp sugar

Follow directions above. Serves 6 to 8.

Indian Pudding

1 gallon milk	2 cups cornmeal
^{1}/$_4$ lb. margarine	1 Tbsp cinnamon
6 eggs	1 Tbsp vanilla
1^3/$_4$ cups sugar	^{1}/$_2$ lb. raisins
2 cups molasses	

Reserve 1 cup of milk and heat remainder with margarine. In large bowl, beat eggs and reserved milk. Mix in sugar, molasses, cornmeal, cinnamon and vanilla. Combine with warmed milk and stir in raisins. Bake pudding in large kettle 2 hours at 350°. Stir often during first 30 minutes of baking to prevent cornmeal sticking. Serves 24.

Family-sized recipe for Indian Pudding on page 127.

Tapioca Pudding

4 quarts milk	1 tsp salt
$^1/_4$ lb. margarine	2 cups tapioca
10 eggs, separated	1 tsp vanilla
2 cups sugar	

Heat milk and margarine in double boiler. In large bowl, beat egg yolks with $1^1/_2$ cups sugar, salt and tapioca, then add to heated milk. Cook 5 minutes, stirring well. Remove from heat and add vanilla. Beat egg whites with remaining sugar until stiff and fold into hot pudding. Serves 20 to 24.

Family-Size Tapioca Pudding:

2 eggs, separated	$^1/_4$ tsp salt
2 cups milk	1 tsp vanilla
2 Tbsp sugar	$^1/_4$ cup sugar
2 Tbsp tapioca	

Mix in saucepan, egg yolks (lightly beaten), milk, 2 Tbsp sugar, tapioca and $^1/_4$ tsp salt. Cook over low heat, stirring constantly, until mixture boils. Remove from heat, cool, and stir in vanilla. Beat 2 egg whites with $^1/_4$ cup sugar until fluffy. Fold into pudding. Serves 6 to 8.

Steamed Pudding with Sweet Sauce

We serve this pudding with Thanksgiving dinner at Moody's.

1 pint breadcrumbs	1 egg, beaten
$^1/_4$ cup molasses	1 tsp baking soda
1 cup milk	2 Tbsp flour
1 cup raisins, chopped	

Combine all ingredients, mix well and pour into greased 1 lb. coffee can. Cover can with tinfoil or wax paper and steam 2 hours. Remove pudding from can, slice and top with Sweet Sauce. Makes 8 servings.

Sweet Sauce:

1 egg   ¹/₃ cup margarine, melted
1 cup sugar   1 tsp vanilla

Combine all ingredients and beat for 2 to 3 minutes. Pour over steamed pudding slice when serving.

Moody's Homemade Ice Cream

We made all of our own ice cream until 1943 or '44, when we stopped because of sugar rationing. This was the recipe that Mom used for the mix that the boys carried to the ice cream room at the back of the garage to freeze.

After the individual flavors were made for the diner, the rest was poured into a "run-over" can that we used for family desserts. Dad also bottled his own milk then, so there were bottle caps in there too. There was a hole in the floor near the ice cream room. We would sneak in, on hot summer days, to sample the run-over can, using bottle caps as spoons. To keep from getting caught, we'd toss the used caps through the hole in the floor. When they tore the building down, there was a huge pile of bottle caps under the building. Dad always wondered where they came from.

We now use Round Top ice cream, made close by, in Damariscotta, Maine.

27 egg yolks   7 quarts milk
10 cups sugar   2 quarts cream
3 Tbsp gelatin   4 (12 oz.) cans evaporated milk
4 tsp salt

Beat egg yolks; add sugar, gelatin and salt, and beat again. Heat milk in double boiler. When hot, stir in egg mixture and cook until batter coats spoon. Add cream, evaporated milk and flavoring. Freeze using an ice cream maker.

Divide the mix for smaller portions to make several different flavors. We made many flavors. Be creative.

RECIPES FROM THE PASTRY KITCHEN

All muffin recipes make 2 dozen muffins.

Bran Muffins

6 cups All-Bran cereal
5 cups milk
4 eggs
1¹/₃ cups shortening, melted

5 cups flour
2 tsp salt
2 cups sugar
4 Tbsp baking powder

Combine bran and milk in mixing bowl, let set 20 minutes, then beat
with mixer or by hand. Add eggs and beat. Stir in melted shortening by
hand. Sift together dry ingredients and add to batter. Put batter into
greased muffin tins, filling ³/₄ full and bake 20 minutes at 400°.

Blueberry Muffins

6 cups flour
4 Tbsp baking powder
1¹/₂ tsp salt
1 cup sugar

3 eggs
3 cups milk
1 cup shortening, melted
2 cups blueberries

Mix together flour, baking powder, sugar and salt. Set aside. Beat eggs; add
milk and combine with dry ingredients. Add melted shortening and mix.
Dust blueberries with flour and fold into batter. Fill greased muffins tins ³/₄
full. Bake 20 minutes at 400°.

Date Muffins

6 cups flour
4 Tbsp baking powder
1¹/₂ tsp salt
1 cup sugar

3 eggs
3 cups milk
1 cup shortening, melted
1¹/₄ cups date filling

Sift dry ingredients. In large bowl, beat eggs, add milk and combine with
dry ingredients. Mix thoroughly and stir in melted shortening. Fold in
date filling and fill greased muffin cups ³/₄ full. Bake 20 minutes at 400°.

Pineapple Muffins

6 cups flour
4 Tbsp baking powder
1½ tsp salt
1 cup sugar
3 eggs

2 cups milk
1 cup pineapple juice
1 cup shortening, melted
2 (20 oz.) cans crushed pineapple, drained

Sift together dry ingredients and set aside. Beat eggs in separate bowl. Add milk and pineapple juice and combine with dry ingredients. Mix thoroughly. Stir in melted shortening and fold in crushed pineapple. Pour batter into greased muffin tins, ³/4 full and bake 20 minutes at 400°.

Homemade Doughnuts

Our bakers arrive by 4:30 A.M., and the first order of the day is the mixing of the doughnuts and the preparation of the dough for cinnamon rolls. Five to six dozen doughnuts are hot and ready when the breakfast crowd arrives.

Plain Doughnuts

4 eggs
2 cups sugar
3 Tbsp margarine, melted
1 tsp vanilla
2 cups milk

5½ cups flour
4 tsp baking powder
3 tsp nutmeg
1¼ tsp salt

Beat eggs with sugar, margarine and vanilla. Mix in milk, 3 cups flour and remaining dry ingredients. Add remaining flour until dough is soft enough to handle. Let dough rest for 30 minutes. Turn onto floured surface and roll out. Cut with doughnut cutter and fry in hot oil (350°). Makes 32 doughnuts.

Chocolate Doughnuts

2 eggs
1¼ cups sugar
3 Tbsp margarine, melted
1½ tsp vanilla
1 cup buttermilk, or sour milk
1 tsp baking powder

4 cups flour
1 tsp salt
1 tsp baking soda
⅛ tsp ginger
2 heaping Tbsp cocoa

Beat together eggs, sugar, margarine and vanilla. Add milk and stir. Sift dry ingredients and add to batter. Let dough rest 30 minutes. Roll dough on floured surface and cut with doughnut cutter. Fry in hot oil (350°). Makes 15 doughnuts.

Brownies

1^1/$_3$ cups margarine
8 sqs. unsweetened chocolate
4 cups sugar
8 eggs
2 tsp vanilla

1 tsp salt
2 tsp baking powder
2^2/$_3$ cups flour
1 cup chopped nuts

Melt together chocolate and margarine; set aside to cool. In large bowl, cream sugar and eggs until creamy, then add cooled chocolate. Beat. Mix in vanilla, salt, baking powder, flour and chopped nuts. Pour into ungreased 12 x 18 inch baking pan and bake 25 to 30 minutes at 375°.

All cupcake recipes make 16 to 18 cupcakes.

Chocolate Buttermilk Cupcakes
Ethelyn Barbour-Baker

2 cups sugar
2 eggs
^{2}/$_3$ cups oil
3 cups flour
2 tsp baking soda

1 tsp salt
^{3}/$_4$ cup cocoa
1 cup boiling water
1 cup buttermilk

Beat sugar and eggs until fluffy, slowly add oil. While this beats, mix flour, baking soda, salt and cocoa. Add boiling water to egg mixture, then add buttermilk. Add flour mixture and mix briefly. Line muffin tins with cupcake papers. Fill with batter ^{3}/$_4$ full. Bake 20 minutes at 375°.

Peanut Butter Cupcakes

2 cups white sugar
5 eggs
$^3/_4$ cup oil
1 cup peanut butter
2 tsp vanilla

4 cups flour
2 tsp salt
1 Tbsp plus 2 tsp baking powder
2 cups milk

Beat sugar and eggs in mixer until fluffy. Slowly add oil, then add peanut butter and vanilla. Mix dry ingredients and add with milk to egg mixture and beat briefly. Line muffin tins with cupcake papers. Fill papers $^3/_4$ full with batter. Bake 20 minutes at 375°.

Banana Cupcakes

$1^1/_2$ cups oil
3 cups sugar
4 eggs
2 tsp vanilla
2 cups bananas, mashed

$^1/_2$ cup milk
4 cups flour
2 tsp baking soda
1 tsp salt

Combine and cream oil, sugar, eggs and vanilla. Add milk, bananas, flour, baking soda and salt. Mix well. Pour batter into muffin tins filled with cupcake papers, filling $^3/_4$ full. Bake 15 to 20 minutes at 400°.

Whoopie Pies

3 cups sugar
4 eggs
$^3/_4$ cup margarine, melted
$^3/_4$ cup oil
3 cups milk
1 tsp vanilla

6 cups flour
$1^1/_2$ tsp baking powder
$4^1/_2$ tsp baking soda
1 tsp salt
$1^1/_2$ cups cocoa

Beat sugar and eggs until fluffy, then add oil, melted margarine and vanilla. Mix dry ingredients together and stir lightly into mixture. Drop by spoonfuls on greased baking sheet and bake at 350° for 15 minutes. Fill with whoopie pie filling. Makes 24 large pies.

See pages 145 and 157–59 for family-size recipes and various fillings. (Note that you'll need to double or triple the filling recipes for this diner-size quantity of whoopie pies.)

MOODY'S PIES

Unless the instructions say otherwise, all recipes make one 9-inch pie.
We still use Mom's Pie Crust recipe, which you can find on page 134.

Basic Cream Filling

3 cups milk
1/4 cup margarine, or butter
2 eggs
1 cup sugar

3 Tbsp flour
3 Tbsp cornstarch
pinch of salt
1 tsp vanilla

Heat milk and butter in double boiler until milk steams. Beat eggs and
sugar until real fluffy. Add flour, cornstarch, salt and vanilla to egg mixture. Add to hot milk, stirring constantly with wire whip until thickened.
Pour into cooked pie shell.

May be mixed lightly in electric mixer after thickened to make extra smooth.

Banana Cream:
Line cooked pie shell with sliced bananas. Cover with cream filling.

Coconut Cream:
Add 1 cup shredded coconut to cream filling. Pour into cooked pie shell.

Peanut Butter Cream:
1 cup peanut butter to hot filling, stirring until well blended. Pour into
cooked pie shell.

Top all pies with whipped cream.

Chocolate Cream Pie

3 cups milk
1/4 cup margarine
1 cup sugar
3 eggs
4 level Tbsp cornstarch

4 level Tbsp flour
3 Tbsp cocoa, or 2 Tbsp cocoa
    plus 1 (2 oz.) square bittersweet
    chocolate
1 tsp vanilla

Heat milk and margarine in double boiler. (If using chocolate squares,
melt them in the milk.) Mix sugar, cornstarch, flour, cocoa and eggs, and
pour into heated milk. Stir well until thickened. Add vanilla and stir.
Pour into cooked pie shell and chill until firm. Top with whipped cream.

Blueberry Pie

4 cups blueberries
1 Tbsp flour
1 cup sugar
cinnamon, or nutmeg to taste

dash of salt
2 Tbsp margarine
2 Tbsp milk

Pour blueberries into unbaked 9-inch pie shell. Mix dry ingredients and pour over berries. Dot with margarine. Cover with top crust that has been dusted with flour and brushed with milk. Bake 35 minutes at 350°.

Moody's Four-Berry Pie

1 cup strawberries
1 cup blackberries
1 cup blueberries
1 cup raspberries

1 cup sugar
2 Tbsp tapioca
dash of salt
$1/2$ tsp cinnamon

Put berries in unbaked 9-inch pie shell. Mix sugar, tapioca, salt and cinnamon and pour over berries. Dot with butter. Cover with top crust. Bake at 325° for 1 hour.

If possible, use wild Maine blueberries. Large, cultivated ones do not have as much flavor.

Strawberry-Rhubarb Pie

3 cups strawberries, sliced
2 cups rhubarb, cut-up

2 Tbsp tapioca
$1^1/4$ cups sugar

Place rhubarb and strawberries in unbaked 9-inch pie shell. Mix sugar and tapioca and spread over fruit. Dot with butter. Cover with top crust and bake at 350° for 1 hour.

Fresh Strawberry Pie
Betty Dyer

1¹/₂ cups water
³/₄ cup sugar
2 Tbsp cornstarch
1 Tbsp margarine

1 tsp vanilla
1 (3 oz.) pkg. strawberry Jell-O
1 quart fresh strawberries

Combine, water, sugar and cornstarch in saucepan, and cook over
Medium heat until thickened. Remove from heat and add margarine,
vanilla and Jell-O. Mix and cool slightly. Slice strawberries and arrange in
baked pie shell. Pour Jell-O mixture over strawberries and chill until firm.
Top with whipped cream when serving.

We use this recipe when fresh strawberries are available during the summer.

Moody's Lemon Meringue Pie
Arlene Eugley-Baker

1¹/₂ cups sugar
¹/₂ cup cornstarch
¹/₄ tsp salt
¹/₂ cup cold water

¹/₂ cup lemon juice
4 eggs, separated
2 Tbsp butter
1¹/₂ cups boiling water

Using a large saucepan, mix together sugar, cornstarch and salt. Use wire
whisk and gradually blend in cold water, then lemon juice until mixture is
smooth. Separate eggs and add beaten egg yolks, blend vigorously. Add
butter and gradually stir in boiling water, stirring constantly. Gradually
bring mixture to a full boil, stirring over high heat. Boil slowly for 1
minute. Pour hot filling in cooled baked 9-inch pie shells. Makes two
pies.

Never-Fail Meringue:

1¹/₂ Tbsp cornstarch
3 Tbsp cold water
¹/₃ cup boiling water

4 egg whites
²/₃ cup sugar
pinch of salt

Blend cornstarch and cold water in a small pan and add hot water. Cook
until clear and thick. Cool completely. Beat egg whites until foamy.
Gradually add sugar and beat until stiff at low speed; add salt. Gradually
beat in cold cornstarch mixture. Beat at high speed for 1 minute. Cover
lemon filling with meringue mixture and bake in 350° oven for 8 to 10
minutes, until browned.

Moody's Custard Pie

8 eggs
1 cup sugar
1 tsp nutmeg

1 level Tbsp flour
1 tsp salt
5 cups milk

In large bowl, beat eggs with flour, salt, sugar and nutmeg. Stir in milk and pour batter through strainer into unbaked deep 9-inch pie shell. Bake 15 minutes at 400°, then reduce heat to 325° and bake 25 to 30 minutes or until pie is set.

Moody's Walnut Pie

$^3/_4$ cup margarine, melted
$1^1/_2$ cups sugar
9 eggs
3 heaping Tbsp flour
$^3/_4$ tsp salt

$1^1/_2$ tsp vanilla
$2^1/_2$ cups dark corn syrup
2 cups milk
2 cups chopped walnuts

In large bowl, beat together melted margarine, sugar, eggs, flour, salt, vanilla and corn syrup. Beat well, then stir in milk. Spread 1 cup nuts in each uncooked 9-inch pie shell. Pour batter over nuts. Bake 30 to 40 minutes at 350°. Makes two pies.

Appetizers

Chili con Queso
Charlene Ward

1 cup onion, finely chopped
1 tsp shortening
1 large ripe tomato, finely chopped
2 med. green chilies, finely chopped

2 Tbsp chili powder
$^1/_2$ tsp oregano
$^1/_2$ tsp salt
$^3/_4$ lb. grated Cheddar cheese

Sauté onion in melted shortening, add tomatoes, green chilies, spices and salt. Cook 10 minutes over low heat. Add cheese and heat until melted. If necessary, add a little milk for desired consistency. Pour dip into fondue pan or chafing dish to keep it warm. Serve with tortilla chips.

Cheese Ball I
Gail Kennedy

2 (8 oz.) pkgs. cream cheese
1 (4 oz) jar port wine cheese spread
1 (5 oz.) jar blue cheese spread

1 tsp Worcestershire sauce
$^1/_4$ cup chopped nuts

Bring all ingredients to room temperature and combine. Mix well. Shape cheese into a ball and then roll in nuts. Chill. Serve with crackers.

Cheese Ball II
Charlene Ward

1 (8 oz.) pkg. cream cheese
1 (4 oz.) jar pineapple cheese spread
1 (4 oz.) jar Cheddar cheese spread

1 (4 oz.) jar pimento cheese
$^1/_4$ cup onion, chopped
$^1/_4$ cup walnuts, chopped

Bring all ingredients to room temperature and combine. Mix well and shape cheese into a ball. Roll in nuts and chill before serving.

Lorraine's Beef Dip
Rebecca Little

1 lb. ground beef
$^1/_2$ cup onions, chopped
1 clove minced garlic
1 (8 oz.) can tomato sauce
$^3/_4$ tsp oregano, crushed

$^1/_4$ cup catsup
1 tsp sugar
1 (8 oz.) pkg. cream cheese
$^1/_3$ cup grated Cheddar cheese

Cook together ground beef, onions and garlic. Drain meat and stir in remaining ingredients, except cheeses. Simmer 10 minutes and remove from heat. Add cheeses and stir. Serve warm with nacho chips.

Taco Dip
Anne Braley

1 (8 oz.) pkg. cream cheese, softened
1 cup sour cream
1 pkg. taco seasoning mix

1 cup lettuce, shredded
1 tomato, diced
1 cup grated Cheddar cheese

Combine cream cheese, sour cream and taco seasoning. Beat well and spread in 9 x 13 inch pan. Top with lettuce, tomato and grated cheese. Serve with taco chips.

Chutney Spread
Dorothy Bruns Moody

2 (8 oz.) pkgs. cream cheese
$^1/_2$ cup toasted almonds, chopped
$^1/_2$ cup prepared chutney

1 tsp curry powder
$^1/_2$ tsp dry mustard

Combine all ingredients and blend until smooth. Pour into small bowl and chill until firm. Serve with crackers.

Pickles & Relish

Dad always had a large garden, and making our own pickles and relish was a summer tradition. Our cellar had many cupboards to hold the results of the summer bounty for those long winter days. It is certainly easier today to just pick up all these things at the local supermarket, but the comfort of knowing you were prepared for winter by the works of your own hands was very satisfying.

For those of you who are fortunate enough to have a garden, we offer these recipes.

Bread and Butter Pickles I
Nancy Moody Genthner

25 medium cucumbers, sliced
10 medium onions, sliced
$^1/_2$ cup salt
3 cups vinegar
2 cups sugar

2 tsp mustard seed
2 tsp celery seed
$^1/_2$ tsp turmeric
$^1/_2$ cup water

Slice cucumbers and onions into large bowl and sprinkle each layer with salt. Let stand 2 to 3 hours and drain. In large kettle, combine vinegar, sugar, spices and water and bring to a boil. Add cucumbers and cook 5 minutes. Pack in sterilized jars and seal while hot.

To make Bread and Butter Pickles in smaller quantities, use the recipe below:

Bread and Butter Pickles II
Thelma Kennedy

4 quarts cucumbers
4 small onions
$^1/_2$ cup salt
$^1/_2$ cup sugar

3 cups vinegar
1 Tbsp white mustard seed
1 tsp celery seed
1 tsp turmeric

Slice cucumbers and onions into bowl and sprinkle with salt. Add water to cover and let stand overnight. Drain. In large kettle, combine and boil sugar, vinegar and spices. Bring to boil and add cukes and onions. Cook 15 minutes longer. Seal in hot, sterilized jars.

Ripe Cucumber Pickles
Bertha Moody

3 quarts large ripe cucumbers, peeled
2 large sweet red peppers
3 medium onions
3 cups sugar

2 cups vinegar
3 Tbsp salt
1 Tbsp whole mixed pickling
   spices

Peel large cucumbers, remove seeds and cut in cubes. Put peppers and onions through food grinder. Combine cucumbers, onions, and red peppers in large kettle and sprinkle with salt. Let stand for 3 to 4 hours, or overnight.

Drain and combine with vinegar and sugar in large kettle. Put pickling spices in spice bag or tie in white cloth and add to kettle. Bring to a boil and simmer until cucumbers become transparent and tender. Seal in sterilized jars while hot.

This was a favorite recipe of my Mom's. The pickles are delicious as a side dish with baked beans, or right out of the jar. Use this on the cucumbers in your garden that grow too big!

Freezer Pickles
Avis Maloney

2 quarts cucumbers, sliced and unpeeled
2 medium onions, thinly sliced
1¹/₂ cups sugar

¹/₂ cup vinegar
1 heaping tsp salt

Combine cucumbers, onions and salt in large bowl, and let set 6 hours or more. Boil together sugar and vinegar and cool in refrigerator until thickened. Drain cucumbers and onions, rinse with cold water. Combine with thickened syrup and pour into freezer containers. Freeze. Ready to eat in 5 days.

Cucumber Relish
Nellie Moody Jones

4 quarts cucumbers, peeled and cubed | 1 tsp turmeric
4 large onions | 4 tsp salt
2 sweet red peppers | 3 cups sugar
2 green peppers | 3 cups vinegar
1 tsp mustard | 4 tsp mustard seed

Finely chop cucumbers, onions and peppers. Combine with remaining ingredients in large kettle and simmer until vegetables become transparent. *Do not boil.* Seal in hot, sterilized jars.

Hot Dog Relish
Pat Caldwell

1 sweet red pepper | $^1/_2$ cup salt
1 green pepper | $1^1/_2$ cups sugar
2 onions | $1^1/_2$ cups vinegar
2 cucumbers | 1 handful whole mixed pickling
2 cups green tomatoes | spices, tied in cloth bag

Chop peppers, tomatoes, cucumbers and onions. Add salt and let stand overnight, or at least 4 hours. Rinse thoroughly in cold water and drain. Combine all ingredients in large kettle and cook 45 minutes over moderate heat. Remove spice bag. Seal relish in hot, sterilized jars.

Beet Relish
Nellie Moody Jones

1 quart beets, cooked | 1 Tbsp salt
1 quart cabbage | $^1/_2$ tsp black pepper
$^1/_2$ cup horseradish | vinegar
1 cup sugar

Finely chop beets and cabbage, as for piccalilli. Combine with remaining ingredients in large kettle and mix with vinegar until consistency of relish. Put in sterilized jars and seal.

Zucchini Relish
Nellie Moody Jones

3 green peppers, diced
2 sweet red peppers,
5 cups diced onions
1 cup diced celery
10 cups diced zucchini
1 cup pickling salt

2 tsp turmeric
1 Tbsp dry mustard
3 Tbsp celery seed
6 cups sugar
5 cups white vinegar
3 Tbsp cornstarch

Combine red and green peppers, onion, celery and zucchini, in a large bowl. Sprinkle with salt and let stand overnight. Drain vegetables and rinse thoroughly in colander. In large kettle, combine remaining ingredients with vegetables and bring to a rolling boil. Reduce heat and simmer gently for 20 minutes. Seal in hot, sterilized jars.

Soups

Bubbling Squeak
Thelma Moody

1¹/₄ cups frozen peas
1¹/₄ cups potatoes, diced
1¹/₄ cups carrots, diced

1 lb. ground beef
1 cup onion, chopped
1 can tomato soup

Cook peas and drain, reserving liquid. Boil potatoes in same water as peas, plus enough water to cover potatoes. When potatoes are nearly cooked, add carrots. Cook ground beef and onions in frying pan. Add tomato soup to cooking vegetables; then stir in cooked beef and onions. Bring to boil, add peas and simmer 5 minutes.

Cheeseburger Chowder
Lynne Moody Weister

1 lb. ground beef
¹/₂ cup celery, finely chopped
¹/₄ cup onion, chopped
2 Tbsp green pepper, chopped
3 Tbsp flour

¹/₂ tsp salt
4 cups milk
1 Tbsp beef bouillon
1 cup sharp shredded Cheddar
   cheese

Brown ground beef in large skillet or saucepan. Add celery, onion and green pepper. Cook until vegetables are tender. Blend in flour and salt, add milk and bouillon. Cook and stir over low heat until thickened. Add cheese and heat until cheese melts. Serves 4 to 6.

Hamburger Soup
Peggy Jones

1 lb. ground beef
1 cup potatoes, chopped
1 cup celery, chopped
1 cup onion, chopped
1 cup carrots, chopped
1 cup cabbage, chopped
1 1/2 quarts water

1 (28 oz.) can crushed tomatoes
1/4 cup long-grain rice, uncooked
1/2 tsp basil
1/2 tsp thyme
1 bay leaf
salt and pepper

Brown ground beef and drain. In large saucepan, combine ground beef with remaining ingredients, except cabbage. Cover and simmer 45 minutes, adding cabbage in last 10 minutes of cooking. Add salt and pepper to taste.

Hearty Lentil Sausage Stew
Cathy Robbins

1 1/2 lbs. sausage
2 medium onions, chopped
2 cloves of garlic, minced
6 carrots, sliced thin
4 cups lentils
4 beef bouillon cubes

1 tsp marjoram
2 (28 oz.) cans whole tomatoes
    with juice
1 box frozen chopped spinach
salt to taste
8 to 10 cups water

Brown sausage in saucepan, remove meat and pour off all but 1/4 cup of the drippings. Add the onions, garlic and carrots and cook 5 minutes. Add lentils, bouillon cubes, browned sausage, marjoram, tomatoes, spinach, salt and water. Simmer about 1 hour or until tender. Serve with Parmesan cheese and Tabasco sauce.

Taco Soup
Jean Moody

1 lb. ground beef
1 large onion, diced
3 (16 oz.) cans Mexican-style chili beans, undrained
1 (16 oz.) can whole kernel corn, undrained
1 (16 oz.) can chopped tomatoes

1 (15 oz.) can tomato sauce
1^1/$_2$ cups water
1 (4^1/$_2$ oz.) can chopped green chilies
1 pkg. taco seasoning mix
1 pkg. ranch-style salad dressing mix

Cook ground beef and onion in large Dutch oven over Medium heat. Drain off fat. Stir in beans, corn, tomatoes tomato sauce, water, chilies, taco seasoning mix and salad dressing mix. Bring to a boil; reduce heat and simmer, uncovered, for 15 minutes. Garnish with sour cream, crumbled tortilla chips and shredded cheese.

Corn Chowder
Anne Braley

1 small piece salt pork, diced
^{1}/$_2$ cup onion, chopped
3 Tbsp margarine
2 cups boiling water

2 cups potatoes, diced
1 tsp salt
1 (10 oz.) can creamed corn
1 (12 oz.) can evaporated milk

Sauté diced salt pork and chopped onion in margarine. Add water, potatoes and salt. Bring to a boil and simmer until potatoes are tender. Add creamed corn and evaporated milk. Let chowder sit 30 minutes before serving to blend flavor.

Add an extra can of creamed corn, if you like.

Potato Cheese Soup
Christine Reed

4 cups potatoes, chopped
^{1}/$_3$ cup celery, chopped
^{1}/$_3$ cup onion, chopped
3 cups chicken broth

2 cups milk
salt and pepper to taste
2 (8 oz.) cups shredded Cheddar cheese

Cook potatoes, celery and onions in chicken broth until tender. Puree potato mixture in food processor. Return to sauce pan, add milk, salt and pepper. Add cheese and heat until melted.

Sausage Tortellini Soup
Jean Moody

1 lb. Italian sausage links
1 large onion, chopped
2 cloves minced garlic
3 cans beef or chicken stock
2 cans diced tomatoes
1 (8 oz.) can tomato sauce
1 cup dry red wine

3 carrots, sliced
1 Tbsp sugar
1^1/$_2$ tsp mixed Italian seasoning
2 small zucchini, sliced
1 (9oz.) pkg. refrigerated
   cheese-filled tortellini
^{1}/$_2$ cup shredded Parmesan cheese

Remove sausage meat from casings. (Use either sweet or hot sausage.) In large pot, cook sausage meat with onion and garlic over medium heat, stirring until meat is no longer pink. Drain fat from pan. Stir in stock, diced tomatoes, tomato sauce, wine, carrots, sugar and Italian seasoning. Bring to a boil; reduce heat and simmer for 30 minutes. Skim off any fat. Add zucchini and tortellini and simmer for 10 minutes. Ladle into bowls and sprinkle with Parmesan cheese.

Minestrone Vegetable Soup
Cathy Robbins

3 Tbsp olive oil
1 lb. lean Italian sweet sausage
1 large onion, chopped
2 (28 oz.) cans Italian plum tomatoes,
   with juice
salt to taste
1 tsp black pepper
2 tsp sugar
2 tsp dried basil
6 large carrots, sliced thin

6 celery stalks, sliced thin
2^1/$_2$ quarts chicken broth, or
10 cups water and 10 chicken
   bouillon cubes
1 (20 oz.) can white cannellini
   beans
1 (20 oz.) can red kidney beans
1 to 2 cups cooked Arborio rice
   or long-grain brown rice

In large stockpot, heat olive oil over low heat and add sausage (that has been removed from its casing and crumbled), cooking until the sausage loses pinkness (3 to 5 minutes). Add onion and sauté until translucent. Add tomatoes with juice, salt, pepper, sugar and basil. Cook sauce uncovered, stirring frequently for 15 minutes. Add carrots and celery, stirring frequently, for an additional 5 minutes. Pour in chicken broth and bring to a boil over high heat. As soon as soup reaches a boil, turn heat to low, cover pot and simmer, stirring frequently, until vegetables are cooked, about 45 minutes. Drain both kinds of beans and stir in. Add rice. Cook, covered, for an additional 5 minutes. Remove from heat and let soup rest for 2 hours before serving so that all the flavors meld together. Reheat over low heat, serve with freshly grated Parmesan or Romano cheese.

May also add 2 or 3 minced cloves garlic, frozen chopped spinach, and frozen, cut green beans.

Margaret's Beef Stew
Mary Olson

2 Tbsp margarine, melted
2 Tbsp flour
$^1/_2$ cup catsup
3 cups boiling water
1 onion, diced

4 or 5 carrots, sliced
3 or 4 potatoes, diced
salt and pepper to taste
1 lb. cubed stew beef

Combine margarine and flour in stew pot or crockpot. Add catsup and boiling water. Add beef and vegetables. Bring to a boil and simmer until beef is tender. In crockpot, simmer on Low all day.

Marge's Mulligatawny Soup
Nancy Moody Genthner

4 or 5 chicken thighs
1 clove minced garlic
2 Tbsp margarine
$^1/_2$ cup long-grain rice, uncooked
1 cup carrots, sliced

$^1/_2$ cup celery, chopped
$^1/_2$ cup onion, diced
$^1/_2$ cup green pepper, chopped
3 or 4 chicken bouillon cubes
$^1/_2$ cup cabbage, shredded

Place chicken in kettle and cover with water. Cook until tender. Remove chicken from bones and cut into cubes. Reserve broth. (To remove fat from broth, put broth in refrigerator overnight, spoon off hardened fat and continue with recipe.)

In large saucepan, sauté garlic in margarine. Add rice, carrots, onions, celery, green peppers. Sauté lightly. Heat chicken broth to boiling, add bouillon cubes. Add vegetables and rice to broth and cook on medium heat for 30 minutes. Add cut-up chicken. Add shredded cabbage and cook for 10 more minutes. Let stand for 30 minutes to enhance flavor.

Tuna and Broccoli Soup
Hannah Flagg

1/4 cup margarine	1/4 tsp white pepper
3 Tbsp minced onion	dash cayenne pepper
3 Tbsp flour	4 cups milk
1 1/4 tsp salt	1 (10 oz.) pkg. frozen broccoli
1/2 tsp celery salt	1 (6 oz.) can tuna, drained and
1/2 tsp sage	flaked

Melt margarine in heavy saucepan, add onion and cook until tender. Blend in flour, salt, celery salt, peppers and sage. Heat until bubbling, gradually add milk and stir constantly to boiling. Add broccoli and cook over low heat 10 to 15 minutes, stirring occasionally. Fold in tuna and heat through. Serves 6.

Pea Soup, Newfoundland Style
Debbie Moody Bellows

2 quarts water	1 carrot, sliced
1 lb. dried yellow split peas	1 cup potato, diced
1 small onion, chopped	1 cup ham, in bite-size pieces
1 cup turnip, diced	salt and pepper

Combine all ingredients in large kettle. Bring to a boil and then simmer for 1 1/2 to 2 hours. Serve with warm corn bread.

Haddock Fish Chowder
Nancy Moody Genthner

3 medium potatoes	1 can evaporated milk
1/3 cup butter or margarine	1/2 cup half and half
1 large onion, chopped	salt and pepper to taste
1 lb. fresh or frozen haddock fillets	

Peel and dice potatoes. Melt half the butter in kettle, sauté onions and then add haddock. Cover with water and bring to a boil, cooking 10 minutes or until fish flakes apart. Remove fish from water, add potatoes and cook 10 minutes or until potatoes are tender. Add fish, evaporated milk, and half and half. Heat on medium heat until hot. Do not boil. Add remainder of butter to broth. Let stand a while before serving to enhance flavor.

~⊂ Salads ⊃~

Aunt Bertha's Salad

Naomi Walker

1 quart cranberries
1 large orange, peeled
1 large apple
1 (8¹/₂ oz) can crushed pineapple

2 cups sugar
3 cups water, hot
1 (6 oz.) pkg. orange Jell-O
1 (6 oz.) pkg. mixed fruit Jell-O

Grind together cranberries, orange and apple, including peel. Add pineapple and sugar and let set 2 hours. Dissolve Jell-O in hot water, add fruit and chill until firm.

Strawberry Salad
Nancy Moody Genthner

2 (3 oz.) pkgs. strawberry Jell-O
2 cups boiling water
1 (10 oz.) pkg. frozen strawberries

1 (8¹/₂ oz.) can crushed pineapple
1 cup whole cranberry sauce

Dissolve Jell-O in boiling water. Add strawberries and stir frequently until strawberries are thawed. Mix together cranberry sauce and pineapple and add to strawberry mixture. Refrigerate all day or overnight until firm.

Fruit Salad
Jan Jones

1 (16 oz.) can fruit cocktail
1 (6 oz.) can pineapple chunks
1 (6 oz.) can mandarin oranges

1 cup miniature marshmallows
1 cup sour cream
¹/₄ cup nuts or shredded coconut

Drain all fruit and mix with marshmallows and sour cream. Let set in refrigerator overnight before serving.

Orange-Pineapple Surprise
Joan Moody

2 (3 oz.) pkgs. orange or mixed-fruit
   Jell-O
1³/₄ cups boiling water
1 (14 oz.) jar cranberry-orange relish

1 (20 oz.) can crushed pineapple
³/₄ cup celery, diced
¹/₂ cup chopped walnuts or pecans

Dissolve Jell-O in boiling water; add relish and mix well. Stir in pineapple, celery and nuts. Pour into 6-cup mold. Chill until firm and unmold on lettuce-lined plate. Serve with mayonnaise dressing if desired.

Strawberry Pretzel Salad
Mary Olson

2 cups pretzels, crushed
3 Tbsp sugar
³/₄ cup margarine, melted
¹/₂ cup powdered sugar
1 (8 oz.) pkg. cream cheese

1 medium pkg. Cool Whip
2 cups miniature marshmallows
1 (6 oz.) pkg. strawberry Jell-O
2¹/₂ cups boiling water
1 (10 oz.) pkg. frozen strawberries

Mix first three ingredients in 9 x 13 inch pan. Bake at 350° for 15 minutes. Cool. Cream softened cream cheese and add powdered sugar. Fold Cool Whip into cheese mixture. Add marshmallows. Spread over baked crust. Dissolve gelatin in hot water. Stir in strawberries. Chill until slightly thickened. Spread over cheese layer. Chill.

Martian Salad
Christine Reed

1 box pistachio pudding
1 (6 oz.) can pineapple chunks
1 container Cool Whip

2 cups miniature marshmallows
¹/₄ cup chopped nuts (optional)

Pour pudding mix into bowl; add pineapple and juice. Add remaining ingredients and stir well. Refrigerate several hours before serving.

Mom's May Day Salad
Judy Moody Beck

2 cups cottage cheese
1 (3 oz.) pkg. lime Jell-O
1 (3 oz.) pkg. lemon Jell-O
2¹/₂ cups crushed pineapple

2 cups fruit cocktail
¹/₂ cup chopped nuts
1 (12 oz.) container Cool Whip

Mix cottage cheese with dry Jell-O; add drained fruit and nuts. Fold in Cool Whip. Any combination of fruits and Jell-O can be used.

Green Molded Salad
Janet Braley

1 (3 oz.) pkg. lime Jell-O
1 cup boiling water
¹/₂ cup cold water
1 (8 oz.) pkg. cream cheese, softened

1¹/₂ cups miniature marshmallows
1²/₃ cups crushed pineapple
¹/₂ cup chopped nuts, optional

Dissolve Jell-O in boiling water, then add cold water. Mix cream cheese into Jell-O, using egg beater. Chill 1¹/₂ to 2 hours. Fold in marshmallows, pineapple and nuts. Pour into mold and refrigerate until firm.

Roberta's Sinful Salad
Judy Moody Beck

1 (6 oz.) pkg. strawberry Jell-O
1 cup boiling water
1 cup bananas, mashed
2 (10 oz.) pkgs. frozen strawberries,
  thawed and drained

1 (20 oz.) can crushed pineapple,
  drained
1 cup chopped walnuts
2 cups sour cream

In medium bowl, dissolve Jell-O in boiling water. Cool. Fold in bananas, strawberries, pineapple and walnuts, stir. Pour half the Jell-O into an 11 x 7 inch pan and refrigerate until set, about 1 hour. Keep remaining Jell-O at room temperature. Spread sour cream over partially-set Jell-O and cover with remaining Jell-O. Cover and refrigerate until set.

Potato Salad
Hannah Flagg

4 cups potatoes, cooked and cubed
$1/4$ cup oil
2 Tbsp vinegar
3 eggs, hard-boiled and chopped

$1/2$ cup mayonnaise
1 cup celery, diced
2 to 3 Tbsp onion, chopped
salt and pepper to taste

Marinate potatoes 1 to 2 hours in oil and vinegar. Add remaining ingredients and mix well. Season with salt and pepper. Garnish with parsley or hard-boiled egg.

Grammie Buck's Mashed Potato Salad
Anne Braley

12 to 15 large potatoes
10 eggs, hard-boiled
4 cups mayonnaise
1 Tbsp celery salt

$1^1/2$ Tbsp onion powder
salt and pepper to taste
parsley or paprika for garnish

Peel and boil potatoes until tender. Drain and mash while still hot. Dice 9 of the boiled eggs and combine with hot potatoes. Add mayonnaise, celery salt, onion powder, salt and pepper, and mix well. Grate remaining egg over top of salad. Garnish with parsley or paprika.

Lemon-Ginger Chicken Salad
Dorothy Bruns Moody

$1/2$ cup mayonnaise
$1/4$ cup sour cream
1 Tbsp sugar
$1/2$ tsp lemon rind
1 Tbsp lemon juice
$1/2$ tsp ground ginger

$1/2$ tsp curry powder
2 cups chicken, cooked and cubed
1 cup green grapes
1 cup celery, sliced
$1/4$ cup toasted almonds

In large bowl, mix together mayonnaise, sour cream, sugar, lemon rind, lemon juice, ginger and curry powder. Fold in chicken, grapes and celery. Toss to coat. Chill before serving. Serve on cantaloupe halves and sprinkle with toasted almonds.

Greek Pasta Salad
Dorothy Bruns Moody

¹/₃ cup olive oil
1 Tbsp vinegar
2 Tbsp sugar
5 large tomatoes
3 medium cucumbers
1 green pepper
1 onion
1 tsp salt
¹/₄ to ¹/₂ cup mushrooms, sliced
¹/₄ to ¹/₂ cup broccoli and zucchini,
   cut up (optional)

¹/₂ tsp salt
¹/₄ tsp dry mustard
¹/₄ tsp paprika
¹/₄ tsp celery seed
1 garlic clove minced,
   or ¹/₈ tsp garlic salt
1 (4 oz.) can black olives
1 tsp oregano
4 oz feta cheese
1 (1 lb.) box curly pasta

Combine oil, vinegar and sugar; mix and refrigerate 2 hours. Cook the pasta and cool. Slice vegetables and combine with remaining ingredients and pasta in large bowl. Cover with cold oil mixture and mix together.

Lemon-Garlic Dressing
Judy Moody Beck

¹/₃ cup lemon juice (2 lemons),
   fresh-squeezed
²/₃ cup olive oil

1 Tbsp minced garlic
1 tsp garlic salt and parsley mix

Combine all ingredients in container and shake to mix well.

Mexican Taco Salad
Linda Moody Davis

¹/₂ lb. ground beef
1 (12 oz.) can kidney beans
1 small onion, chopped
1 pkg. taco chips, crushed

2 medium tomatoes, chopped
1 head lettuce, shredded
1 cup shredded Cheddar cheese
¹/₃ cup Catalina salad dressing

Cook ground beef and drain. Drain kidney beans. Combine all ingredients and mix well. Top with Catalina dressing. Serves 8.

Marilyn's Cheese and Macaroni Salad
Debbie Moody Bellows

1^1/$_2$ cups macaroni, uncooked
1 (10-oz.) pkg. frozen peas
^{1}/$_3$ cup sweet relish
^{3}/$_4$ cup Miracle Whip or mayonnaise
2 cups shredded Cheddar cheese

^{1}/$_2$ cup onion, chopped
^{1}/$_2$ cup celery, chopped
salt
^{1}/$_2$ head lettuce, chopped
^{1}/$_3$ cup bacon bits

Cook, drain and rinse macaroni. Rinse peas to separate. Mix relish into Miracle Whip (or mayonnaise). Mix macaroni, peas, cheese, onions, celery and salt. Coat mixture with blended Miracle Whip and relish. Just before serving, toss with lettuce and bacon bits. For special occasions, substitute 1 can tiny shrimp for 1 cup of the cheese.

Lorraine's Barbecue Sauce
Rebecca Little

2 cups catsup
1 tsp pepper
scant ^{3}/$_4$ cup sugar

1 Tbsp onion powder
1^1/$_2$ cups vinegar
8 tsp Worcestershire sauce

Combine all ingredients in saucepan and simmer 10 to 15 minutes.

Breads & Muffins

Apricot-Oatmeal Muffins

Dorothy Bruns Moody

1 egg
1 cup buttermilk
$^1/_2$ cup brown sugar
$^1/_3$ cup shortening
1 cup flour

1 tsp salt
1 tsp baking powder
$^1/_2$ tsp baking soda
1 cup dry oatmeal
$^1/_2$ cup dried apricots, chopped

In large bowl, beat egg, buttermilk, brown sugar and shortening. Sift all dry ingredients, except oatmeal, and add to batter. Mix thoroughly. Fold in apricots and oatmeal and stir until moistened. Spoon batter into 12 greased muffin cups, $^2/_3$ full. Bake 15 to 20 minutes at 400°.

Blueberry Muffins

Nancy Moody Genthner

$^1/_4$ cup margarine
$^1/_2$ cup sugar
1 egg
2 cups flour

3 tsp baking powder
$^1/_2$ tsp salt
1 cup milk
$1^1/_2$ cups blueberries

Cream together margarine and sugar, add egg and beat well. Mix in dry ingredients, then stir in milk. Dust blueberries with flour and fold into batter. Spoon into 12 greased muffin tins, $^2/_3$ full, and bake 20 minutes at 375°.

Blueberry-Oatmeal Muffins
Mary Olson

$^{1}/_{2}$ cup rolled oats
$^{1}/_{2}$ cup orange juice
$1^{1}/_{2}$ cup flour
$^{1}/_{2}$ cup sugar
$^{1}/_{2}$ cup oil

1 egg, slightly beaten
$1^{1}/_{4}$ tsp baking powder
$^{1}/_{2}$ tsp salt
$^{1}/_{4}$ tsp baking soda
1 cup blueberries

In a large bowl, combine oats and orange juice. Stir well. Add flour, sugar, oil, egg, baking powder, salt and soda. Mix well. Dust blueberries with flour and stir in. Spoon into greased muffin tins. Bake at 400° for 18 to 22 minutes. If desired, sprinkle top of muffins before baking with 2 Tbsp sugar mixed with $^{1}/_{4}$ tsp cinnamon.

Molasses Bran Muffins
Nancy Moody Genthner

1 cup All-Bran cereal
1 cup dry oatmeal
$1^{1}/_{2}$ cups milk
1 egg

$^{1}/_{2}$ cup molasses
1 cup flour
1 tsp baking soda
1 tsp salt

Mix bran and oatmeal with milk and let set until soft. When soft, stir in egg and molasses, then add dry ingredients. Pour batter into greased muffin tins, $^{2}/_{3}$ full and bake 20 minutes at 350°. (Batter will be quite runny, and it makes a very moist muffin.)

Granola Bran Muffins
Judy Moody Beck

4 cups bran flakes
2 cups granola
2 cups milk
$^{1}/_{2}$ cup oil
$^{1}/_{3}$ cup honey

2 eggs
2 cups flour
2 Tbsp baking powder
1 tsp salt

Combine cereal, granola, milk, oil, honey and eggs in bowl; mix well, let stand 10 minutes. Stir to break up cereal. Combine flour, baking powder and salt, and add to cereal mixture. Stir just until moist. Put in muffin pans and bake. For variety, may add raisins, dried cranberries or dates. Bake at 400° for 20 minutes. Makes 24 muffins.

Doughnut Muffins
Nancy Little

1 egg	2 tsp baking powder
$^1/_3$ cup oil	$^1/_2$ tsp salt
$^1/_2$ cup milk	$^1/_2$ tsp nutmeg
$1^1/_2$ cups flour	$^1/_2$ cup sugar

Beat egg in large bowl, add oil and milk and beat again. Sift dry ingredients and stir into batter. Pour batter, half-filling 12 greased muffin
tins. Top each muffin with pat of margarine and dash of cinnamon sugar
(2 Tbsp sugar and $^1/_4$ tsp cinnamon). Bake 20 minutes at 400°.

Mom's Molasses Doughnuts
Nellie Moody Jones

2 eggs	$^1/_2$ tsp cinnamon
$^3/_4$ cup sugar	1 tsp nutmeg
$^1/_2$ cup molasses	$3^1/_2$ cups flour
2 Tbsp shortening, melted	1 rounded tsp baking soda
1 cup buttermilk or sour milk	$^3/_4$ tsp salt
$^1/_4$ tsp ginger	

Beat eggs until light, add sugar and beat well. Add molasses, shortening
and buttermilk. Sift dry ingredients and add to batter. Chill several hours.
Roll out dough on floured surface to $^1/_2$-inch thickness. Cut with doughnut cutter and fry in hot fat (350°).

Grammy's Chocolate Doughnuts
Pat Caldwell

$3^1/_2$ cups flour	2 eggs
dash of salt	$1^1/_4$ cups sugar
pinch of ginger	1 tsp vanilla
3 heaping Tbsp cocoa	3 Tbsp shortening, melted
1 heaping tsp baking soda	1 cup buttermilk or sour milk

Sift together dry ingredients, except sugar, and set aside. Beat eggs in large
bowl, add sugar, melted shortening, buttermilk and vanilla. Mix thoroughly. Stir in dry ingredients and mix. Do not overmix. Let batter rest 30
minutes. On floured surface roll out dough to $^1/_2$-inch thickness. Cut with
doughnut cutter and fry in hot fat (350°). To make plain doughnuts, omit
cocoa and add 1 tsp nutmeg.

Mom's Brown Bread
Debbie Moody Bellows

1 cup dry oatmeal
3 cups graham flour
3 cups buttermilk or sour milk

¹/₂ tsp salt
1 cup molasses
3 tsp baking soda

Combine all ingredients in large bowl and mix well. Pour batter into greased coffee cans, ²/₃ full. Cover top with tin foil and steam 2 hours. Remove from cans and slice warm.

Mom always made this to serve with baked beans on Saturday night.

Brown Bread
Anne Braley

1 cup graham flour
1 cup cornmeal
1 cup white flour
1 tsp salt

1¹/₂ tsp baking soda
1 cup molasses
2 cups buttermilk or sour milk

Combine dry ingredients. Add buttermilk and molasses and mix thoroughly. Pour batter into two well-greased 1 lb. coffee cans. Cover with wax paper and secure with elastic band. Steam 2 hours.

Best-Ever Banana Bread
Judy Moody Beck

1 cup sugar
¹/₂ cup margarine
2 eggs, beaten
1 cup bananas, mashed
2 cups flour

1 tsp baking powder
¹/₂ tsp salt
¹/₄ cup buttermilk or sour milk
¹/₂ cup chopped nuts

Cream together margarine and sugar; add eggs and banana and mix well. Combine dry ingredients and add to batter, alternately with buttermilk. Fold in nuts. Bake in loaf pan 1 hour at 350°.

Peg's Pumpkin Bread
Nancy Moody Genthner

1³/4 cups flour
¹/4 tsp baking powder
1 tsp baking soda
1 tsp salt
¹/2 tsp cloves
¹/2 tsp cinnamon
¹/2 tsp allspice
¹/2 tsp nutmeg
1¹/2 cups sugar
¹/2 cup oil
2 eggs
1 cup pumpkin, cooked
¹/3 cup water

Sift together dry ingredients, except sugar. In large bowl, combine sugar and oil. Add eggs and pumpkin and mix thoroughly. Stir in dry ingredients and water. Mix well and pour batter into a greased and floured loaf pan. Bake 1 hour at 350°.

Rhubarb Bread
Gail Kennedy

1 cup rhubarb, chopped
2³/4 cups flour
1¹/2 cups packed brown sugar
1 tsp baking soda
1 tsp salt
1 egg
1 cup buttermilk
¹/2 cup oil
1 tsp vanilla
2 Tbsp flour
2 to 3 tsp margarine
2 to 3 tsp granulated sugar

Toss rhubarb with 2 Tbsp flour and set aside. In large bowl, stir together flour, brown sugar, baking soda and salt. In separate bowl, combine egg, buttermilk, oil and vanilla. Mix well and stir in dry ingredients. Fold rhubarb into batter and pour into two greased 8 x 4 loaf pans. Top each loaf with pats of margarine and sprinkle with sugar. Bake 55 minutes at 350°.

Strawberry Bread
Judy Moody Beck

3 cups flour
1 tsp baking soda
1 tsp salt
1 Tbsp cinnamon
4 eggs, beaten

$1^1/_2$ cups oil
2 cups sugar
2 cups fresh or frozen strawberries,
   sliced
$1^1/_2$ cups chopped walnuts

Sift dry ingredients, except sugar, and set aside. In large bowl, beat together eggs, oil and sugar. Add dry ingredients and mix well. Fold in strawberries and nuts, and pour into 2 greased loaf pans. Bake 1 hour at 350°.

Zucchini Bread
Jean Moody

3 eggs
1 cup oil
2 cups sugar
2 tsp vanilla
2 cups zucchini, coarsely shredded
1 ($8^1/_2$ oz.) can crushed pineapple,
   drained

3 cups flour
2 tsp baking soda
1 tsp salt
$^1/_2$ tsp baking powder
$1^1/_2$ tsp cinnamon
$^3/_4$ tsp nutmeg
1 cup nuts, raisins or dates

Beat eggs in large bowl and add oil, sugar and vanilla. Beat until thick and foamy. Stir in zucchini and pineapple. Sift and add dry ingredients until just blended. Fold in nuts or raisins and pour batter into two 5 x 9 inch greased loaf pans. Bake 1 hour at 350°.

Zucchini-Orange Bread
Mary Olson

4 eggs
$1^1/_2$ cups sugar
$^3/_4$ cup oil
$^2/_3$ cup orange juice
$3^1/_4$ cups flour
$1^1/_2$ tsp baking powder

1 tsp salt
2 tsp orange peel, grated
$2^1/_2$ tsp cinnamon
$^1/_2$ tsp cloves
2 cups zucchini, shredded
$^1/_2$ cup chopped nuts

In large bowl, beat together eggs and sugar. Add oil and orange juice and mix well. Sift dry ingredients and add to egg batter. Stir thoroughly and fold in zucchini and nuts. Pour batter into 2 greased and floured loaf pans. Bake 45 to 55 minutes at 350°.

When cooled, top this bread with a glaze of 1 cup powdered sugar combined with 2 to 3 Tbsp orange juice, if you like.

Blueberry Crumb Coffee Cake
Gail Kennedy

2 cups flour
$^1/_2$ tsp salt
3 tsp baking powder
$^1/_2$ cup sugar
$^1/_2$ cup shortening

1 egg, beaten
$^1/_2$ cup milk
2 tsp lemon juice
2 cups blueberries

Crumb Topping:
$^1/_3$ cup sugar
$^1/_3$ cup flour

$^1/_2$ tsp cinnamon
$^1/_4$ cup margarine

Sift flour, salt and baking powder and set aside. In large bowl, cream shortening and sugar, add egg and beat until light. Stir milk into eggs, alternating with dry ingredients. Mix well and pour batter into 8-inch greased pan lined with wax paper. Pour lemon juice over blueberries and spread over batter. In small bowl, combine sugar, flour and cinnamon. Add margarine and mix until small crumbs form. Sprinkle topping over blueberries. Bake 55 to 60 minutes at 350°. Serve warm.

Cranberry Coffee Cake
Nellie Moody Jones

$^1/_2$ cup margarine
1 cup sugar
2 eggs
1 tsp baking powder
1 tsp baking soda
2 cups flour

$^1/_2$ tsp salt
1 cup sour cream
1 tsp almond extract
1 (16 oz.) can whole-cranberry sauce
$^1/_2$ cup chopped walnuts

In large bowl, cream margarine and sugar, add eggs and beat well. Mix together dry ingredients and add alternately with almond flavoring and sour cream and mix thoroughly. Spread half the batter in greased, 9-inch tube pan and top with half the cranberry sauce. Add remaining batter and top with remaining sauce. Sprinkle with nuts and bake 55 minutes at 350°.

Prune-Apricot Coffee Cake
Ona Moody

3/4 cup prunes, chopped
3/4 cup apricots, chopped
3/4 cup sugar
3/4 cup softened shortening
2 eggs

2 cups flour
2 tsp baking powder
3/4 cup milk
1 tsp vanilla

Topping:

2/3 cup packed brown sugar
1 Tbsp flour
6 Tbsp margarine or shortening,
   melted

1 Tbsp cinnamon
1/2 cup chopped nuts

Let prunes and apricots stand in hot water 5 minutes. Drain. In large
bowl, cream sugar and margarine, add eggs and mix well. Mix together dry
ingredients, then add alternately with milk and vanilla. Stir and fold in
prunes and apricots. Pour 1/3 of the batter into greased and floured tube
pan; cover with 1/3 of the topping. Sprinkle with 1/3 of the nuts and
melted margarine. Repeat layers. Bake 55 minutes at 350°.

Mom's Biscuits
Nellie Moody Jones

4 cups flour
2 Tbsp baking powder
1/2 tsp salt

1/2 cup shortening
2 cups milk

Sift together dry ingredients. Cut shortening into dry ingredients until
mixture resembles fine meal. Add milk and stir together. Turn dough onto
floured surface and roll out. Cut with biscuit cutter, place on pan and
bake at 450° 12 to 15 minutes, until dry when pulled apart.

*You can substitute orange juice for the milk; it gives a nice flavor and is good
for those with milk allergies.*

Shredded Wheat Bread
Judy Moody Beck

4 cups water
2 cups milk
5 cups shredded wheat cereal
2 tsp salt
1 cup oil
1^1/$_2$ cups molasses

4 Tbsp yeast
1 cup water, warm
7^1/$_2$ cups King Arthur white flour
6 cups whole wheat flour
2 cups rye flour

Heat water and milk to boiling. Pour over shredded wheat cereal and soak 30 minutes. Add salt, oil, and molasses and stir. Mix yeast in warm water and stir into mixture. Mix in 6 cups white flour. Then add 6 cups whole wheat flour, 2 cups rye flour and 1^1/$_2$ cups of white flour. Mix well. Cover and let rise until double in size. Punch down, divide into 6 loaves. Knead and roll out each loaf in a rectangle, roll up like a jelly roll, pinch ends and tuck under loaf and place in greased bread pan. Cover and let rise until double. Only bake three loaves at a time. The second three will be fine rising while the first three bake. Bake 25 to 30 minutes at 350°. If top gets too brown, bake at 325° for 30 to 32 minutes.

You can substitute 8 cups of whole wheat flour and 1^1/$_2$ cups white flour for the rye flour.

If you are fortunate enough to have a Universal Bread Maker from the early 1900s, use it to mix the dough. I have my mom's [Bertha Moody's] and use it every week.

Oatmeal Bread
Susan Moody

^{1}/$_2$ cup water, warm
1 yeast cake or 2 pkg. dry yeast
2 cups milk, scalded
1 cup oatmeal

^{1}/$_2$ cup molasses
2 tsp salt
1 Tbsp shortening
4^1/$_2$ to 5 cups flour

Mix water with yeast and set aside. Allow milk to cool, then mix with oatmeal, molasses, salt, shortening and yeast. Add flour until dough is easy to handle. Add more flour as necessary. Turn dough onto floured surface and knead 3 to 4 minutes. Place in greased bowl to rise until doubled in volume. Knead again and divide dough. Shape into loaves or place in two greased loaf pans and let rise again. Bake loaves 20 to 30 minutes at 350°. Brush tops of loaves with butter after cooking.

Chris's Oatmeal Bread
Chris Reed

1 cup rolled oats
2 cups boiling water
2 pkgs. dry yeast
$1/3$ cup lukewarm water

2 tsp salt
2 Tbsp margarine, softened
$1/2$ cup molasses
$51/2$ to 6 cups flour

Put oats in large bowl and cover with boiling water. Let stand 30 minutes, until the water has cooled to warm. Sprinkle yeast into lukewarm water and let stand 5 minutes. Do not stir. Meanwhile, add salt, margarine and molasses to soaked oats. Stir yeast and pour into oats. Stir in 2 cups flour, then add 3 to 4 cups more. Work in the last of the flour by hand. Knead dough on floured surface and place in greased bowl to rise until doubled in bulk (about 2 hours). Punch down dough and divide. Shape into loaves and place in 2 well-greased loaf pans. Cover and let rise 1 hour. Bake 30 minutes at 350°.

Coffee Bread
Marion Whitmore

2 pkgs. active dry yeast
$1/2$ cup lukewarm water
$1/2$ cup margarine
2 cups milk, scalded
4 eggs, beaten

1 cup sugar
1 tsp vanilla
22 cardamom seeds, finely pounded,
    or 1 Tbsp ground cardamom
7 cups flour

Dissolve yeast in warm water. Add margarine to scalded milk. In large bowl, beat eggs and sugar until spongy, add vanilla and cardamom. Mix well and add yeast and milk. Stir in enough flour to make dough easy to handle. Turn dough onto floured surface and knead. Place in warmed, greased bowl and let rise until doubled in bulk. Divide dough into three equal parts to make three loaves. Divide dough again and braid. Place braided loaves on greased baking sheet to rise. Bake 20 minutes at 350°.

Nissua (Finnish Bread)

Dot Aho Moody

3/4 cup margarine
3/4 cup sugar
2 tsp salt
2 cups milk, scalded
3 pkgs. dry yeast

1 cup water, warm
9 or 10 cardamom seeds, crushed
6 eggs, beaten
10 to 11 cups flour

Stir margarine, sugar and salt into scalded milk, and set aside to cool. In small bowl, dissolve yeast in warm water. When milk is lukewarm, add crushed cardamom seeds, dissolved yeast and beaten eggs. Stir in 6 cups of flour and knead about 10 minutes. Knead in remaining flour and let rise until doubled in bulk (about 1 1/2 hours). Punch down and let dough rise 30 minutes more. Punch down again and divide into four equal lengths and braid to make 4 loaves. Let rise 1 hour. Beat 1 egg and brush on loaves, then sprinkle with sugar. Bake 20 minutes at 350°.

Decorate for the holidays with powdered sugar icing, red and green glazed cherries, and nuts, and omit the brushed egg.

Irish Freckle Bread

Andrea Moody Newbert

1 small potato, pared
1 cup raisins
2 pkgs. dry yeast
1/2 cup water, very warm
2 eggs, beaten

1/2 cup sugar
1/2 cup margarine, melted
4 1/2 cups flour
1 tsp salt
1/2 tsp cinnamon

Cook potato in 1 cup water for 15 minutes. Leave potato in water and mash. Measure and add water, if necessary, to make 1 cup potato. Stir raisins into potato and let cool. In large bowl, sprinkle yeast into very warm water, and stir until yeast is dissolved. Add mashed potato and raisins. Mix in beaten eggs, sugar, and melted margarine. Stir in 2 cups flour, salt and cinnamon and mix until batter is smooth. Stir in remaining flour to make stiff dough. Turn out on floured surface and knead dough until smooth and elastic. Place in large, greased bowl, turning to coat with shortening. Cover bowl with cloth and let dough rise until doubled in size. Punch down and knead several times. Divide dough and shape into loaves. Place in two greased loaf pans and let rise 45 minutes. Bake 35 minutes at 350°, until golden brown and loaves make a hollow sound when tapped. Brush with glaze (next page).

Freckle Bread Glaze:

$^1/_2$ cup light corn syrup and $^1/_2$ cup water, heated to boiling and simmered 5 minutes. Remove from heat and stir in $^1/_2$ tsp vanilla. Brush generously onto each loaf.

Dark Yeast Rolls
Nancy Moody Genthner

$^3/_4$ cup water
$^3/_4$ cup milk
$^1/_2$ cup shortening
$^1/_2$ cup rolled oats
$^1/_2$ cup All-Bran cereal
1 tsp salt

3 Tbsp molasses
2 Tbsp brown sugar
2 pkgs. dry yeast
$^1/_3$ cup lukewarm water
4 cups flour

Combine $^3/_4$ cup water and $^3/_4$ cup milk in saucepan and bring to boiling. In large bowl, combine shortening, oats, bran, salt, molasses and brown sugar. Pour boiling water-milk mixture over these ingredients and let set until lukewarm. Dissolve yeast in $^1/_3$ cup lukewarm water and add to mixture. Stir. Add flour 1 cup at time and mix. Cover and let dough rise until doubled in bulk. Turn dough onto floured surface, knead lightly and shape into rolls. Place in greased muffin tins or greased baking sheet and let rise again. Bake 20 minutes at 425°.

Refrigerator Rolls
Doris Moody Eaton

2 cups boiling water
$^1/_2$ cup shortening
$^1/_2$ cup sugar
1 tsp salt
2 pkgs. dry yeast

$^1/_4$ cup lukewarm water
1 tsp sugar
2 eggs, lightly beaten
8 cups flour

Mix boiling water, shortening, sugar and salt in large bowl. Stir until shortening melts. Dissolve yeast in lukewarm water and add 1 tsp sugar. When shortening and water mix is lukewarm, stir in yeast. Add eggs, and 4 cups flour. Beat thoroughly and add remaining flour. Mix, but do not knead; the dough should be soft. Cover and store in refrigerator. To bake, remove dough from refrigerator, shape into rolls and let rise until doubled in bulk. Bake 15 to 20 minutes at 400°.

Sixty-Minute Rolls
Nancy Moody Genthner

2 pkgs. dry yeast
$^1/_4$ cup lukewarm water
$1^1/_4$ cups milk
3 Tbsp sugar

$^3/_4$ tsp salt
$^1/_4$ cup butter or margarine
$3^1/_2$ to $4^1/_2$ cups flour

Dissolve yeast in lukewarm water. Combine milk, sugar, salt and half the margarine in small saucepan and heat until lukewarm. Add yeast, and stir in flour. Cover dough and let rise in warm place 15 minutes. Turn dough onto floured surface and pat to $^1/_2$-inch thickness. Cut with 2-inch biscuit cutter and place on greased baking sheet. Brush with remaining melted margarine and fold dough in half. Let rise 15 minutes more. Bake 10 to 12 minutes at 425°.

Mom's Pizza Dough
Christine Beck Reed

$1^1/_3$ cups very warm water
1 Tbsp yeast
2 Tbsp oil

$^1/_2$ tsp garlic salt
$^1/_2$ tsp basil
3 cups flour

Dissolve yeast in water. Add remaining ingredients and stir. Place on greased cookie sheet and spread to edges with moistened finger tips. Add sauce, cheese and favorite toppings and bake at 450° for 15 to 20 minutes. (For a puffy crust, put toppings on dough and let it rise for 30 minutes before baking.)

Peggy's Pizza Dough
Debbie Moody Bellows

1 pkg. dry yeast ($2^1/_2$ tsp)
1 cup warm water
1 tsp sugar

1 tsp salt
2 Tbsp oil
$2^1/_2$ cups flour

Dissolve yeast in warm water. Stir in remaining ingredients. Beat vigorously—20 strokes. Allow dough to rest for 5 minutes. Knead, roll out and shape to greased pizza pan. Top with sauce, cheese and your favorite toppings. Bake in 425° oven for 12 to 15 minutes.

Cherry Peek-a-Boo Rolls
Pat Caldwell

2 pkgs. dry yeast
$1/2$ cup lukewarm water
$1^1/4$ cups milk, scalded
$1/2$ cup sugar
6 Tbsp margarine

2 tsp salt
2 eggs
7 to $7^1/2$ cups flour, sifted
4 Tbsp margarine
1 jar cherry preserves

Dissolve yeast in lukewarm water and set aside. Combine scalded milk and sugar with margarine and salt. Stir. Add dissolved yeast, eggs and 2 cups flour and beat until smooth. Add 5 to $5^1/2$ cups flour to make a soft dough. Turn dough onto floured surface and knead until smooth and satiny.

Place dough in greased bowl and turn once. Cover and let rise until doubled in bulk (about $1^1/2$ hours). Punch down and roll out dough $1/2$-inch thick on lightly floured surface. Spread dough with soft margarine and fold in half. Pinch edges together and again roll dough $1/2$-inch thick. Brush with margarine, fold in half and roll $1/2$-inch thick once more. Cut in $2^1/2$-inch circles and place on greased cookie sheet. Cover and let rise 30 minutes. Depress center of each circle and fill with cherry preserves. Bake 15 minutes at 400°. Frost with powdered sugar icing and decorate with slivered almonds.

Main Course Dishes

Curried Chicken Divan
Cathy Hopler

1 (10 oz.) pkg. frozen broccoli, cooked
3 chicken breasts, cooked and cubed
$^1/_2$ cup mayonnaise
1 tsp lemon juice
$^3/_4$ cup grated Cheddar cheese
1 (10 oz.) can cream of chicken soup
$^1/_4$ to $^1/_2$ tsp curry powder
$^1/_4$ tsp paprika

Place broccoli in greased baking dish and cover with chicken. Combine remaining ingredients, reserving half the cheese, and pour over chicken. Top with remaining cheese and shake paprika on top. Bake, uncovered, 25 to 30 minutes at 350°.

Chicken Divan
Christine Reed

3 chicken breasts
2 (10 oz.) pkgs. frozen broccoli spears
$^1/_2$ cup chicken broth
1 (10 oz.) can cream of chicken soup
$^1/_2$ cup mayonnaise
1 cup sour cream
$^1/_2$ cup grated Parmesan cheese
$^1/_4$ tsp paprika

Boil chicken until tender, remove meat from bone and cut into bite-size pieces. Partially cook broccoli (about 5 minutes). Arrange chicken in a well-greased 12 x 8 inch baking dish and cover with broccoli. Blend broth, soup, mayonnaise and sour cream, and pour over chicken and broccoli. Top with cheese and paprika, and bake 25 to 30 minutes at 350°.

Chicken Gumbo
Norma Moody Dion

4 chicken breasts
2 (10 oz.) cans cream of chicken soup
1³/₄ cups milk
¹/₂ bag seasoned breadcrumbs

1 (10 oz.) can cream of mushroom
  soup
1 (4 oz.) can mushrooms

Cook chicken until tender, remove from bone and cube. Place pieces in a
9 x 13 inch baking pan. Heat cream of chicken soup with 1¹/₄ cups of the
milk and pour over chicken. Top with bread crumbs. Bake at 325° until
hot. Combine and cook undrained mushrooms, mushroom soup and remaining milk. Pour over chicken and serve.

Chicken and Mushrooms in Orange Sauce
Clara Moody Kiener

1 chicken, cut into serving-size pieces,
  or 3 large split chicken breasts
¹/₂ to ³/₄ lb. fresh mushrooms
1 green pepper, sliced
1 yellow onion, sliced
2 rounded Tbsp cornstarch

1 cup orange juice
¹/₂ cup water
¹/₄ cup white wine
1 Tbsp frozen orange juice,
  optional
1 grated orange peel, optional

Lightly salt chicken and broil, skin side up, for 10 minutes. Slice vegetables and spread in bottom of large baking dish. Combine orange juice,
water and wine with cornstarch and cook over low heat until sauce thickens. For a stronger orange flavor, add 1 Tbsp frozen orange juice concen-
trate. Cover vegetables with chicken and top with sauce. Bake 1 hour at
350°, until chicken is tender. Sprinkle with grated orange peel for extra
flavor and garnish.

Lemon Chicken
Peggy Jones

¹/₃ cup flour
1 tsp salt
1 tsp paprika
3 lb. frying chicken
3 Tbsp lemon juice
3 Tbsp oil

1 chicken bouillon cube
³/₄ cup boiling water
2 Tbsp brown sugar
¹/₄ cup green onion, sliced
1¹/₂ tsp grated lemon peel, optional

In a bag, combine flour, salt and paprika. Cut chicken into pieces and brush with lemon juice. Place chicken, two pieces at a time, into bag and shake well. Heat oil in large skillet and brown chicken. Dissolve bouillon cube in boiling water and pour over chicken. Stir in onion, brown sugar, lemon peel and remaining lemon juice. Cook over low heat until tender, about 45 minutes.

Sticky Chicken
Naomi Walker

$^1/_2$ cup sugar
$^1/_2$ cup vinegar

$^1/_2$ cup soy sauce
1 chicken, cut into pieces

Mix and heat sugar, vinegar and soy sauce in deep skillet. Add chicken and cook over moderate heat for 20 minutes, occasionally turning chicken. Cover and cook another 10 minutes. Remove cover and allow sauce to thicken and coat chicken, about 10 minutes. Serve.

Chicken can be marinated overnight before cooking.

Quick Stir-Fried Chicken
Shawn M. Moody

3 Tbsp peanut oil
4 Tbsp soy sauce
$^3/_4$ tsp garlic sauce
2 tsp cornstarch
3 Tbsp cold water
2 cups raw chicken, sliced julienne
1 (6 oz.) pkg. frozen Chinese peapods
1 (8 oz.) can water chestnuts, drained and sliced

$^3/_4$ cup fresh broccoli, chopped
2 oranges, sectioned
1 bunch green onions, trimmed and quartered
$^1/_2$ cup mushrooms, sliced
2 cups cooked rice, or chow mien noodles

Heat oil in wok or skillet over medium heat. When hot, add soy sauce and garlic salt and stir. Combine cornstarch and water, set aside. Add chicken to pan and stir-fry about 3 minutes. Add peapods, water chestnuts and broccoli and stir-fry 2 minutes. Reduce heat, then add orange sections, green onions, mushrooms and cornstarch mix. Stir until thickened and serve over rice or noodles.

Sweet and Sour Chicken
Gail Kennedy

4 to 6 pieces chicken tenders
$^2/_3$ cup sugar
$^1/_4$ cup catsup
$^1/_2$ cup pineapple juice
$^1/_2$ cup white vinegar
2 Tbsp soy sauce

1 Tbsp oil
1 tsp garlic powder
2 Tbsp cornstarch
$^1/_2$ cup cold water
1 cup pineapple chunks

Cook chicken and set aside. In medium saucepan, combine all ingredients except cornstarch, water and pineapple chunks. Heat to boiling. Add cornstarch mixed with water, then add pineapple. Remove from heat and add chicken. Let stand a few minutes before serving over cooked rice.

Very good when prepared ahead and marinated overnight. Just reheat and serve.

Quick Chicken Supper
Anne Braley

2 cups water
2 chicken bouillon cubes
1 (10 oz.) pkg. frozen mixed vegetables

1 can cream of chicken soup
2 cups chopped chicken, or turkey

Boil water and add bouillon cubes. Add vegetables and cook until done. Add soup and chicken, heat until chicken is warmed. Serve over mashed potatoes, noodles or toast.

One of my children's favorite meals.

One-Dish Chicken & Stuffing Bake
Nancy Moody Genthner

$^1/_2$ cup boiling water
1 Tbsp margarine, melted
4 cups cubed seasoned stuffing
4 to 6 skinless, boneless
   chicken breasts

1 (10 oz.) can cream of mushroom
   soup
$^1/_3$ cup milk
1 tsp dried parsley flakes
paprika

Mix water and margarine. Add stuffing, mix lightly. Spoon stuffing across center of baking dish, leaving space on both sides for chicken. Arrange chicken on each side of stuffing. Sprinkle chicken with paprika. Mix soup, milk and parsley. Pour over chicken. Cover and bake at 400° for 30 minutes or until chicken is done.

Ground Turkey Loaf
Shawn M. Moody

1 lb. ground turkey
1 egg
1 pkg. onion soup mix
1 (4 oz.) can mushrooms, drained
1 onion, chopped

3 slices soft wheat bread
$^1/_2$ cup bran
$^1/_4$ cup dry oat bran cereal
barbecue sauce

Combine all ingredients, except barbecue sauce, and shape into a loaf. Place in loaf pan and top with barbecue sauce. Bake $1^1/_2$ hours at 325°.

Turkey and Broccoli Quiche
Sheri Beck

2 cups turkey, cooked and cubed
1 cup shredded Cheddar cheese
$^1/_3$ cup onion, finely chopped
2 cups broccoli, cooked

1 9-inch pie shell, unbaked
4 eggs
2 cups milk
$^3/_4$ tsp salt

Spread turkey, cheese, onion and broccoli in pie shell. Beat eggs slightly, then stir in milk and salt. Pour into pie shell and bake 15 minutes at 425°. Reduce oven to 300° and bake another 30 minutes, or until knife comes out clean when inserted in center of quiche. Let stand 10 minutes before serving.

American Lasagna
Jean Moody

1 lb. ground beef
2 cloves chopped garlic
1 (6 oz.) can tomato paste
$2^1/_2$ cups canned tomatoes
1 tsp salt

$^3/_4$ tsp pepper
$^1/_2$ tsp oregano
1 (8 oz.) pkg. lasagna noodles
8 oz. Swiss or mozzarella cheese
12 oz. cottage cheese

Brown ground beef and garlic in skillet. Add tomato paste, tomatoes and spices, cover and simmer 20 minutes. Half-cook noodles and drain. Coat bottom of 12 x 9 inch baking dish with thin layer of sauce. In baking dish, alternate layers of cooked noodles with cheeses and meat sauce. Bake 20 to 30 minutes at 350°.

Crock Pot Mock Lasagna
Cynthia Hilton

1 (10 oz.) pkg. lasagna noodles
1 lb. ground beef
1 onion, chopped
12 oz. shredded mozzarella cheese
1/2 lb. Italian sausage, optional

12 oz. cottage cheese
1 1/2 Tbsp parsley
1 (32 oz.) jar spaghetti sauce
2 Tbsp grated Parmesan cheese

Break noodles into bite-size pieces, cook and drain. Brown meat and drain. Grease crock pot. Combine all ingredients, except Parmesan cheese, in crock pot and stir lightly. Top with Parmesan cheese and cook 7 to 9 hours on low setting or 3 to 5 hours on high setting.

Vegetable Lasagna
Christine Beck Reed

2 Tbsp olive oil
1 large onion, chopped
1 clove minced garlic
1 tsp Italian seasoning
2 (10 oz.) pkgs. chopped broccoli,
   thawed and drained
1 (10 oz.) can cream of mushroom soup

2 cups shredded Cheddar cheese
1 egg
1 (32 oz.) jar spaghetti sauce
1/2 cup water
2 Tbsp vinegar
9 lasagna noodles, cooked
2 cups shredded mozzarella cheese

Sauté onion, garlic and seasonings in oil until transparent. Stir in broccoli and cook until tender. Remove from heat and stir in soup, Cheddar cheese and egg. Set aside.

In a medium bowl, stir together sauce, water and vinegar. Pour half the sauce into 13 x 9 inch baking dish. Alternate layers of noodles, filling and remaining sauce. Bake 40 minutes at 350°. Sprinkle remaining mozzarella on top and bake 5 more minutes. Let stand 15 minutes before serving.

Pizzasagna
Jolene Millay

9 lasagna noodles
1 (32 oz.) jar spaghetti sauce
pinch of oregano
1 lb. cottage cheese

1 (8 oz.) cup shredded mozzarella
   cheese
2 oz. pepperoni, thinly sliced

Cook and drain lasagna. Spread $^1/_2$ cup spaghetti sauce in 9 x 13 inch baking dish. Top with layer of noodles, sauce, a dash of oregano, cottage cheese and mozzarella. Repeat layers and top with mozzarella and pepperoni. Bake 30 to 40 minutes at 350°, until bubbling. Remove from oven and let stand 15 minutes before serving.

Pizza Rolls
Christine Beck Reed

Filling:

$1^1/_2$ cup spaghetti sauce
Any combination of cooked meats,
    chopped onions, peppers,
    mushrooms, olives, broccoli, etc.

12 oz. mozzarella cheese

Topping:

1 egg yolk

Parmesan cheese

Use recipe for Mom's Pizza Dough on page 93. Prepare dough and divide in two. Roll each piece into a 15 x 10 inch rectangle. Spread sauce to about 1 to inch from edges. Sprinkle with meats and/or veggies, and the mozzarella cheese. Roll, starting at long edge. Place on greased cookie sheet. Brush with egg yolk and sprinkle with Parmesan cheese. Bake at 350° for 20 to 25 minutes until golden brown.

Pesto and Basil Spaghetti Sauce
Brian Moody

3 cups fresh basil leaves
2 to 4 cloves garlic
$^1/_2$ cup nuts
$^3/_4$ cup fresh parsley, chopped
$^1/_2$ cup olive oil

$^1/_4$ cup margarine, melted
salt to taste
$^3/_4$ cup grated Parmesan cheese
juice of $^1/_2$ lemon

Combine all ingredients in food processor and zing into a smooth paste. Serve sauce uncooked over pasta. It is potent and delicious.

Pine nuts, sunflower seeds, walnuts or almonds can be used in this recipe.

Eggplant Parmesan
Cathy Hopler

1 medium eggplant (1 lb.)
$^1/_4$ cup flour
$^1/_2$ tsp salt
1 egg, beaten
$^1/_2$ cup cooking oil

$^1/_3$ cup grated Parmesan cheese
1 (8 oz.) can tomato sauce, or spaghetti sauce
1 (6 oz.) pkg. sliced mozzarella cheese

Peel eggplant and cut into $^1/_2$-inch slices. Combine flour and salt. Dip eggplant into beaten egg, then in flour mixture. Brown in hot oil in large skillet; drain well on paper towels. Place 1 layer of eggplant in 8 x 8 inch (or 1$^1/_2$ qt.) casserole dish, cutting to fit.

Sprinkle with Parmesan cheese, then tomato sauce, then mozzarella. Repeat layers ending with strips of mozzarella on top. Bake casserole, uncovered, in 400° oven for 15 to 20 minutes, or until heated through.

Baked Spaghetti
Christine Beck Reed

4 cups spaghetti sauce
$^1/_2$ lb. black beans, cooked
1 lb. spaghetti, cooked
12 oz. shredded Cheddar cheese

1$^1/_2$ cup ranch dressing, or $^1/_4$ cup water and 1 can cream of mushroom soup combined
$^1/_2$ cup Parmesan cheese

In blender or food processor, combine spaghetti sauce and beans. Set aside. Layer half of spaghetti in greased 9 x 13 inch pan. Spread half of sauce mixture on noodles and top with half of Cheddar cheese. Repeat layer. Spread ranch dressing on top and sprinkle with Parmesan cheese. Bake for 25 minutes at 350°.

You may also leave beans whole and use as a layer.

Loggers' Meatballs
Elizabeth O. Nice

1 lb. ground beef
$^1/_2$ cup dry bread crumbs
$^1/_3$ cup onion, minced
$^1/_4$ cup milk
1 egg

1 tsp parsley, chopped
$^1/_2$ tsp Worcestershire sauce
1 (10 oz.) jar grape jelly
1 (12 oz.) bottle chili sauce

Mix meat, crumbs, onion, milk, egg, parsley and Worcestershire sauce and form meatballs. Put meatballs in pan, bake for 25 minutes at 325°, shaking to turn. Drain off any fat. As they bake, melt grape jelly in pan with chili sauce and keep hot. Place meatballs in casserole dish, pour sauce over meatballs, and serve at once over rice, noodles or other pasta. (Can also be kept hot in crockpot.)

Sweet & Sour Sauce for Meatballs
Nancy Genthner

1 Tbsp oil
$^3/_4$ cup pineapple juice
2 Tbsp cornstarch
1 tsp soy sauce
$^1/_2$ cup water

$^1/_2$ cup sugar
1 small can diced pineapple
1 green pepper, cut in strips
$^1/_4$ cup vinegar

Mix oil with pineapple juice from drained pineapple (add water to make $^3/_4$ cup if necessary). Cook over low heat for a few minutes. Mix cornstarch with soy sauce, vinegar, water and sugar. Add to hot pineapple juice and continue to cook gently, stirring until juice thickens. Add cooked meatballs, pineapple pieces and green pepper strips. Simmer until meatballs are hot.

Braised Short Ribs
Rayetta Flint

4 lbs. short ribs (pork or beef)
2 tsp salt
$^1/_4$ tsp pepper
1 tsp dry mustard
1 Tbsp soy sauce
2 cloves minced garlic

$^1/_2$ cup catsup or tomato paste
$^1/_4$ cup water
$^1/_4$ cup vinegar
1 Tbsp brown sugar
1 medium onion, chopped

Cut ribs into serving portions, figuring $^3/_4$ to 1 lb. per person. In a Dutch oven or large skillet, brown ribs on both sides over high heat. Drain meat and set aside. Combine remaining ingredients and spoon over, around and under ribs. Bake covered for 2 hours at 350°.

Oven Beef or Venison Stew
Faye E. Moody

2 lbs. beef or venison
$^1/_2$ cup celery, chopped
5 small whole onions
7 medium carrots, sliced
4 large potatoes, cubed

1 cup tomato juice
2 Tbsp tapioca
1 Tbsp sugar
2 tsp salt, optional
1 handful fresh parsley, chopped

Cut meat into cubes. Place ingredients in Dutch oven in the following order: meat, celery, onions, carrots and potatoes. Mix together tomato juice, tapioca, sugar and salt and pour over meat and vegetables. Tightly seal Dutch oven with aluminum foil and bake 4 hours at 250°. Resist the temptation to peek, as that will allow steam to escape. Sprinkle with parsley just before serving.

Kielbasa and Rice
Alicia Mortensen

1 Tbsp margarine
1 lb. kielbasa, sliced
$^1/_2$ cup onion, chopped
$^1/_2$ cup green pepper, diced
1 cup celery, sliced
1 large tomato, cubed

$^1/_2$ tsp garlic powder
$^1/_2$ tsp thyme
$^1/_2$ tsp cayenne pepper
2 cups rice, cooked
1 pkg. frozen peapods (optional)

Cook peapods and set aside. Melt margarine in 10-inch skillet and add kielbasa, onions, green pepper and celery. Sauté until vegetables are tender. Add tomatoes and spices and stir. Fold in rice and peapods. Heat through and serve.

Chili Tostada
Cathy Robbins

1¹/₂ lbs. ground beef
1 large onion, chopped
2 (28 oz.) cans tomato sauce
2 cloves minced garlic or
  1 tsp garlic powder

1 (2 lb.) can dark red kidney beans,
  undrained
1 cup green pepper, chopped
3 to 4 Tbsp chili powder

Brown beef and onion; drain excess fat. Add remaining ingredients and simmer for 1 hour. Makes 6 servings.

Optional accompaniments:

1 pint sour cream, 1 lb. shredded sharp Cheddar cheese, shredded lettuce, tortilla chips, 1 cubed avocado, 1 chopped red pepper, sliced black olives, or jalapeños

Judy's Beef Stroganoff
Debbie Moody Bellows

1 lb. London broil
¹/₂ cup onion, chopped
1 (10 oz.) can cream of mushroom soup

1 (4 oz.) can mushrooms
1 cup sour cream
egg noodles

Slice meat into long, thin strips. Sauté chopped onion and meat 5 minutes. Remove meat. Add mushroom soup, mushrooms and sour cream. Add meat, stir and cover. Reduce heat and simmer 30 minutes. Serve over cooked noodles.

Oven Pot Roast
Nancy Moody Genthner

2 lb. rump roast
1 can cream of celery soup
1 pkg. dry onion soup

1 (10 oz.) can cream of mushroom
  soup

Line baking pan with large piece of foil. Place roast on foil, combine cream of celery and cream of mushroom soups and pour over roast. Sprinkle dry onion soup mix over top. Cover with foil and fold the two pieces of foil together, sealing in roast. Bake at 350° for 2 hours.

Steakburgers
Naomi Walker

1 lb. ground beef
$^1/_2$ tsp thyme
$^1/_2$ cup onion, chopped
$^1/_4$ cup catsup
1 egg
pepper

flour
$^1/_2$ cup water
$^1/_2$ cup tomato paste
1 Tbsp mustard
1 beef bouillon cube
1 cup red wine

Combine beef, thyme, onion, catsup, egg and pepper. Shape into patties; coat with flour and fry. Remove patties from skillet and set aside. Add remaining ingredients to skillet and simmer until thickened. Return patties to skillet, coat with sauce and serve.

Baked Pork Chops & Sauerkraut
Nancy Moody Genthner

4 potatoes, peeled and sliced
1 lb. fresh sauerkraut, or 1 can
    sauerkraut

2 Tbsp brown sugar
6 pork chops

Place sliced potatoes in 9 x 13 inch baking dish. Cover with sauerkraut. Sprinkle brown sugar over kraut. Sear pork chops lightly on both sides in skillet. Place chops over sauerkraut. Cover and bake at 350° for 1$^1/_2$ hours.

The Best Meatloaf
Laura Jones

2 lbs. ground beef
2 eggs
$^1/_2$ cup cracker crumbs
$^1/_4$ cup milk

$^1/_2$ cup catsup
1$^1/_2$ tsp salt
$^1/_4$ tsp pepper
1 pkg. onion soup mix

Combine all ingredients in large bowl and mix well. Shape meat in loaf pan and bake 60 to 75 minutes at 350°.

Kaye's Meatloaf
Rebecca Little

1^1/$_2$ lbs. ground beef
1 pkg. onion soup mix
1 cup crushed cornflakes (or oatmeal)
^{1}/$_2$ cup chopped green pepper, optional

2 eggs
^{1}/$_2$ cup milk
^{1}/$_2$ cup Parmesan cheese

Combine all ingredients in large bowl and mix well. Shape meat in loaf pan and bake 60 minutes at 350°.

Meatloaf Roll
Cathy Hopler

1 lb. ground beef
2 eggs
1 cup breadcrumbs
^{1}/$_2$ cup onion, diced
^{1}/$_4$ cup green pepper, diced

1 Tbsp Italian seasoning
^{1}/$_4$ tsp pepper
1 tsp salt
1 (8 oz.) pkg. mozzarella cheese
1 (6 oz.) can tomato sauce

Combine ground beef, eggs, breadcrumbs, onion and green pepper in large bowl. Mix well and add seasonings. Turn meat onto wax paper and flatten to ^{1}/$_2$ inch thick. Cover with sliced cheese and roll up meatloaf like a jelly roll. Place in loaf pan and top with 2 slices of cheese. Cover with tomato sauce and bake 1 hour at 350°.

White Clam Sauce
Dorothy Bruns Moody

^{1}/$_4$ cup olive oil
^{1}/$_4$ cup margarine
3 cloves minced garlic
^{1}/$_2$ cup water
^{1}/$_2$ cup parsley, chopped
pepper to taste

1 tsp oregano
1^1/$_2$ to 2 Tbsp flour
juice from minced clams
2 cups minced clams
2 Tbsp white wine, optional
Parmesan cheese

Heat oil and margarine in skillet, add garlic and cook until translucent. Cool slightly and add water. Stir in parsley, pepper and oregano. Blend together flour and clam juice to make smooth paste and add to skillet. Stir well. Add clams and wine, and heat through. Serve over pasta with Parmesan cheese.

Brian Moody makes a "red" version of this recipe by adding one 8 oz. can of tomato sauce.

Mom's Favorite Shrimp Dish
Judy Moody Beck

1/2 cup onion, chopped
1/2 cup green pepper, chopped
1 can cream of shrimp soup

1 cup sour cream
1/2 tsp curry powder
1 lb. shrimp, cooked

Sauté onion and pepper in olive oil until tender. Add soup and stir until smooth. Stir in sour cream and curry powder and then add cooked shrimp. Heat slowly, stirring often until hot. Serve over rice. Serves 4.

Capesante (a great scallop dish)
Nancy L. Moody

1/4 stick margarine
1 lb. bay scallops
1/2 lb. fresh mushrooms
1 Tbsp ginger
2/3 cup dry white wine

1 Tbsp lemon juice
1 cup whipping cream
salt and freshly ground pepper
3 Tbsp Parmesan cheese

Melt margarine in large, flameproof skillet over medium-high heat. Add scallops, sliced mushrooms and ginger, sauté 2 minutes. Transfer scallops and mushrooms to platter and set aside. Add wine and lemon juice to skillet and cook until liquid is reduced by half. Blend in cream and continue cooking until again reduced by half. Return scallops and mushrooms to skillet, add salt and pepper, and heat through.

Sprinkle with Parmesan cheese and transfer to preheated broiler. Broil until slightly browned. Serve hot with rice.

Baked Fish Fillets
Joan Moody

1 lb. fish fillets
2 Tbsp margarine, melted
2 Tbsp lemon juice
1/2 tsp salt

1/4 tsp pepper
1/4 tsp dried dill weed, optional
2 cups Total cereal, crushed

If fillets are large, cut into serving pieces. Combine margarine and lemon juice, set aside. Mix together salt, pepper and dill weed. Dip each fillet into melted margarine and sprinkle with spices. Coat with crushed cereal. Place fillets in greased, 9-inch pan and bake 25 to 30 minutes at 350°, or until fish flakes easily with fork.

Joan and David spent many winters in Florida where he operated his fishing boat, the Captain Kid. *When my husband, Wayne, and I visited them, Joan cooked many platters of fresh fillets brought home by David and Wayne from the day's catch.*

Baked Fish
Joan Moody

2 lbs. haddock fillets
2 Tbsp margarine
1/4 cup onion, grated

1 egg, beaten
1/2 cup cracker crumbs
1 (10 oz.) can cream of shrimp
 soup

Place fillets in greased baking dish and dot with margarine. Combine remaining ingredients and pour over fish. Bake 45 minutes at 400°.

Mock Lobster Bake
Alicia Mortensen

1 lb. haddock fillets
1/4 cup lemon juice
1/2 cup mayonnaise

1 tsp prepared mustard
1/2 cup Parmesan cheese
paprika

Line 9 x 13 inch pan with foil. Place fillets in pan and sprinkle with lemon juice. Combine mayonnaise with mustard and spread over fish. Sprinkle generously with cheese and dash of paprika to simulate lobster. Bake 20 minutes at 400°.

Dottie's Salmon Loaf
Debbie Moody Bellows

2 (1 lb.) cans salmon, drained
 and flaked
1/2 cup fine breadcrumbs
2 Tbsp margarine, melted
1 tsp parsley flakes

1/2 tsp salt
1 tsp onion flakes
dash of pepper
1 Tbsp chopped pimento, optional
3 eggs, separated

Combine all ingredients except eggs in large bowl and toss lightly. Add beaten egg yolks and mix well. Beat egg whites until stiff and fold into batter. Pour into greased loaf pan and bake 45 minutes at 350°. Serve hot with lemon or white sauce or cold with tart mayonnaise.

Lupiers (a Filipino treat)
Charlene Ward

$^1/_2$ cup onion, chopped
$^1/_2$ cup green pepper, chopped
1 clove crushed garlic
2 Tbsp margarine
2 lbs. ground beef

1 small jar jalapeño relish
pepper to taste
2 pkgs. egg roll wrappers
1 cup grated Cheddar cheese

Sauté onions, green peppers and garlic in margarine. Add ground beef and brown. Drain meat, add jalapeño relish and pepper and simmer 10 minutes. Fill egg roll wrappers each with 2 to 3 Tbsp meat and 2 Tbsp cheese, roll up and deep-fry (350°) until browned.

Subgum
Alicia Mortensen

1 (4 oz.) can sliced mushrooms
$1^1/_2$ cups cooked pork, cubed
2 cups celery, sliced
1 Tbsp margarine
1 cup green pepper, sliced
1 (4 oz.) can water chestnuts, drained
2 cups Chinese cabbage, chopped

$1^1/_2$ cups prepared pork gravy
1 (14 oz.) can bean sprouts
2 tsp soy sauce
1 Tbsp honey
2 to 3 cups chow mein noodles or
    cooked rice
1 pkg. frozen peapods

Cook together mushrooms, pork, celery, green pepper, cabbage and chestnuts in margarine until tender—approximately 10 minutes. Add gravy and stir until thickened. Add honey and stir. Reduce heat and simmer 15 minutes. Add soy sauce, bean sprouts and peapods. Heat through and serve over chow mein noodles or rice.

Chicken, scallops or beef can be substituted for pork.

Enchiladas Supreme
Clara Moody Kiener

2 Tbsp olive oil
8 soft corn tortillas
1 (8 oz.) can enchilada sauce
1 (8 oz.) can tomato sauce
2 cups beef or chicken, cooked

$^1/_2$ (4 oz.) can diced green chilies
$^1/_4$ cup sliced black olives
1 cup sour cream
1 cup grated Cheddar cheese
2 green onions, chopped

Heat oil until hot and dip in one side of tortillas for 5 seconds. Stack and drain. In large skillet, combine and heat sauces. Cover bottom of large baking dish with $^1/_4$ of sauce. Combine meat, chilies and olives in sour cream. Scoop 2 Tbsp meat into each tortilla, fold sides over meat and place in baking dish. Pour sauce over enchiladas and sprinkle with cheese. Top with chopped green onion and bake 35 to 40 minutes at 350° until cheese melts.

Fajitas
Lynne Moody Weister

1 lb. chicken, boned and skinned
5 Tbsp oil
2 Tbsp lemon juice
1 tsp garlic powder
1 tsp seasoned salt
$^1/_2$ tsp oregano

1/2 tsp pepper
1 cup green pepper, sliced
1 cup onion wedges, sliced
1 cup tomato wedges, sliced
$^1/_2$ cup chunky taco salsa
8 hot corn or flour tortillas

In medium bowl, combine meat, 2 Tbsp of the oil, juice and spices. Cover and marinate in refrigerator 6 to 9 hours.

In 10-inch cast iron skillet, heat 3 Tbsp oil until very hot. Sauté half the meat until just browned; add half the peppers and onions, and cook 1 to 2 minutes. Remove from skillet. Add remaining meat and cook, then add remaining peppers and onions, and cook until crisp-tender. Return all meat and vegetables to skillet, add tomato and salsa. Simmer 1 minute, tossing to coat with salsa. Fill tortillas with mixture and enjoy.

Casseroles

Carefree Casserole
Corrine Perkins

$^1/_2$ cup instant rice, uncooked
$^1/_4$ cup onion, chopped
1 Tbsp margarine
1 (10 oz.) can cream of mushroom soup
$1^1/_4$ cups water
2 cups, cooked chicken, diced,
   or tuna, drained and flaked

1 cup peas, cooked
$^1/_2$ tsp salt
$^1/_2$ tsp pepper
$^1/_2$ cup grated Cheddar cheese

Measure rice into $1^1/_2$ qt. casserole. In separate pan, sauté onion in margarine until translucent, blend in mushroom soup and water. Stir in chicken or tuna, cooked peas, salt and pepper. Bring to boil, stirring occasionally. Stir mixture into rice and sprinkle with grated cheese. Cover and bake 20 minutes at 350°. Stir before serving.

Baked Rice Casserole
Judy Moody Beck

1 (10 oz.) can onion soup
1 (10 oz.) can beef consommé
$1^1/_4$ cups long grain rice, uncooked

$^1/_4$ cup margarine
1 (4 oz.) can sliced mushrooms

Place all ingredients in casserole dish, cover with foil. Bake 30 minutes at 350°. Remove foil, stir and bake uncovered 30 minutes longer.

Clam Casserole
Deborah M. Pooley

4 Tbsp margarine
2 cans minced clams, not drained
1 Tbsp dill weed
2 cups saltine crackers, crushed

2 eggs, beaten
2 cups milk
dash of pepper

Melt margarine and coat casserole dish. Combine clams and juice, dill weed, saltines and eggs. Add milk and pepper and pour into casserole. Sprinkle with paprika. Let stand 2 hours, then bake 30 minutes at 350°.

Ruthie's Corn Casserole
Judy Moody Beck

1 can creamed corn
2 eggs, beaten
$^1/_2$ cup oil
1 pkg. Jiffy corn muffin mix

$^3/_4$ cup milk
$^1/_2$ tsp salt
1$^1/_2$ cups shredded Cheddar cheese

Mix all ingredients (except cheese) in 2- or 3-quart casserole dish. Top with cheese and press into mixture slightly. Bake uncovered at 350° for 40 to 50 minutes.

This dish is a big hit everywhere I take it. It doubles well, but needs to cook longer. To double, use 3 eggs and $^3/_4$ cup oil to cut some of the fat.

Chicken and Rice Casserole
Pat Caldwell

1 cup long-grain rice, uncooked
1 (10 oz.) can cream of mushroom soup
4 or 5 chicken breasts

1 pkg. onion soup mix
2 cups water

Combine rice, soups and water and put in greased casserole dish. Top with chicken breasts and bake at 350° for 1 hour.

Chicken or Turkey Bake
Jan Jones

3 cups cooked chicken or turkey
2 cups celery, diced
2 cups long grain rice, cooked
2 (10 oz.) cans cream of chicken soup
4 Tbsp onion, chopped
1 (6 oz.) can sliced water chestnuts
$^1/_2$ cup sliced almonds
1 cup mayonnaise
cornflakes to cover
$^1/_4$ cup margarine, melted

Mix all ingredients, except cornflakes and margarine, and pour into casserole dish. Top with cornflakes and melted margarine. Bake 35 to 40 minutes at 350°.

This casserole can be made a day ahead and stored in the refrigerator. Top with corn flakes before cooking.

Ham & Potato Casserole
Jean Moody

1 (26 oz.) bag frozen shredded potatoes
1 (1 lb.) ham slice, cut in $^3/_4$-inch cubes
2 cans cream of potato, cream of celery, or cream of mushroom soup
1 (10 oz.) pkg. frozen petite peas
$^1/_2$ tsp black pepper
$^1/_4$ cup grated Parmesan cheese
1 cup shredded Cheddar cheese
paprika

Combine shredded potatoes with ham, soup, peas and pepper. Spoon into a lightly greased 13 x 9 inch baking dish. Bake in a 400° oven for 25 minutes. Remove from oven and sprinkle with Parmesan and Cheddar cheeses. Return to oven and bake for an additional 5 minutes, or until cheese melts. Sprinkle with paprika. (This reheats beautifully and tastes even better then.)

Hearty Casserole
Charlene Ward

1 lb. ground beef
2 Tbsp margarine
2 medium onions, thinly sliced
3 or 4 carrots, cut in 1-inch pieces
4 or 5 celery stalks, cut in 1-inch pieces
3 or 4 medium potatoes, quartered
3 Tbsp flour
$^1/_2$ tsp salt
$^1/_4$ tsp pepper
$1^1/_2$ to 2 cups water

Shape ground beef into patties and brown in margarine. Arrange browned patties in bottom of greased casserole. Arrange vegetables in layers over meat. Add flour to pan drippings, add salt and pepper. Add water to make medium gravy; pour over vegetables. Cover and bake 1^1/$_4$ hours at 375°.

Hungry Boys Casserole
Judy Moody Beck

1 lb. lean ground beef
^{1}/$_2$ cup celery, chopped
^{1}/$_4$ cup onion, chopped
^{1}/$_4$ cup green pepper, chopped
^{1}/$_2$ tsp garlic salt

1 lb. can baked beans
^{1}/$_4$ cup catsup
^{1}/$_4$ cup water
^{1}/$_2$ tsp salt

Sauté ground beef with celery, onion and pepper. Remove excess fat and combine with remaining ingredients in a casserole dish. Bake in 400° oven for 30 minutes.

If desired, you may add barbecue sauce, Worcestershire sauce or A-1 sauce to taste. Kidney beans can be added with baked beans for variety. I serve this with Mom's Biscuits (see page 88).

Mom's Macaroni and Cheese
Rachel Little

2 Tbsp margarine
3 Tbsp flour
^{1}/$_2$ tsp salt
dash of pepper

2 cups milk
2 cups shredded Cheddar cheese
2 cups elbow macaroni, cooked
and drained

Melt margarine over low heat, add flour, salt and pepper. Add milk and stir until thickened. Add cheese. When cheese is melted, add to macaroni in 1^1/$_2$-quart casserole. Bake 30 minutes at 350°.

Italian Macaroni and Beef
Jan Jones

1 lb. ground beef
$^{1}/_{4}$ cup green pepper, chopped
$^{3}/_{4}$ cup onion, chopped
1 tsp basil
1 tsp oregano
$^{1}/_{2}$ cup tomatoes, drained
2 Tbsp margarine

3 Tbsp flour
2 cups milk
10 oz. grated Cheddar cheese
salt and pepper to taste
$1^{1}/_{2}$ cups macaroni, cooked and
    drained
Parmesan cheese

Brown meat, onions and pepper. Add basil, oregano and tomatoes, cook 3 minutes. In separate pan, make white sauce with margarine, flour and milk. Add cheese and cook until thickened. Add salt and pepper. Combine meat, macaroni and $^{2}/_{3}$ of sauce in 9 x 13 inch pan. Cover with remaining sauce and sprinkle with Parmesan cheese. Cover and bake 20 to 25 minutes at 400°. Remove cover and cook 2 to 3 minutes longer.

Mom's Spaghetti Casserole
Beverly Eaton

2 Tbsp margarine
$^{1}/_{2}$ cup onion, chopped
1 lb. ground beef
salt and pepper to taste
pinch of oregano

$1^{1}/_{2}$ cups spaghetti, uncooked
2 cups stewed tomatoes
$^{3}/_{4}$ cup water
$^{1}/_{2}$ cup catsup

Sauté onion in margarine in frying pan; add ground beef, salt and oregano. Break spaghetti in pieces to make $1^{1}/_{2}$ cups and place half in 2-quart casserole dish. Cover with half the cooked, ground beef and 1 cup tomatoes. Repeat layers. Mix water and catsup and pour over layers. Cover. Bake 45 minutes at 350° or microwave 22 minutes on High.

Spaghetti Casserole
Donna Fairhurst

2 lbs. ground beef
$^{2}/_{3}$ cup onion, chopped
1 garlic clove, minced
1 tsp oregano
1 tsp salt
$^{1}/_{2}$ tsp pepper

1 qt. spaghetti sauce
1 cup sour cream
2 cups cottage cheese
1 cup grated Parmesan cheese
1 egg
1 lb. spaghetti, cooked and drained

Sauté meat, onion, seasonings in skillet until browned. Stir in spaghetti sauce. Cook for 10 minutes. Mix together sour cream, cheeses and egg. In a greased 9 x 13 inch pan, place a thick layer of sauce on bottom, then ¹/₂ of the cooked spaghetti. Spoon ¹/₂ of the meat mixture on spaghetti and then ¹/₂ of the cheese mixture. Repeat layers, and bake at 375° for 45 minutes.

(Great for preparing ahead of time to pop in the oven later.)

Spaghetti Pie
Linda Moody Davis

6 oz. spaghetti, cooked and drained
2 Tbsp margarine
¹/₃ cup grated Parmesan cheese
2 eggs, well-beaten
1 cup cottage cheese
1 lb. ground beef
¹/₂ cup onion, chopped

¹/₄ cup green pepper, chopped
1 cup stewed tomatoes
1 (6 oz.) can tomato paste
1 tsp sugar
1 tsp oregano
¹/₂ tsp garlic salt
¹/₂ cup shredded mozzarella

Stir margarine into hot spaghetti. Stir in Parmesan cheese and eggs. Spread spaghetti and egg mixture into a 10-inch pie plate, forming "crust." Spread cottage cheese over spaghetti crust. In skillet, cook together beef, onion and green pepper. Drain off excess fat. Stir in tomatoes, tomato paste, sugar, oregano and garlic salt. Heat through. Spread meat and tomato sauce over cottage cheese and bake 20 minutes at 350°. Sprinkle with mozzarella. Return to oven and bake until cheese melts.

Italian Zucchini Casserole
Carol Hallowell

2¹/₂ lbs. zucchini
4 Tbsp margarine
¹/₂ cup onion, chopped
¹/₂ cup green pepper, chopped
1 pkg. spaghetti sauce mix

¹/₂ cup shredded Cheddar cheese
1 (4 oz.) can mushrooms
1 (6 oz.) can tomato paste
1 cup water
Parmesan cheese, grated

Slice zucchini into ¹/₂-inch pieces and drop into boiling water. Cook 4 to 5 minutes and drain. Place zucchini in casserole dish. Sauté onion and green pepper in margarine. Add sauce mix, Cheddar cheese, mushrooms, tomato paste and water. Mix well and pour over zucchini. Sprinkle top with Parmesan cheese. Bake 25 to 30 minutes at 350° or microwave 13 minutes on High, turning once. Let stand 5 to 10 minutes before serving.

Zucchini Casserole
Nellie Moody Jones

2 or 3 medium zucchini, thinly sliced
2 onions, thinly sliced
1 cup shredded sharp Cheddar cheese
2 or 3 tomatoes, chopped
2 Tbsp oil

Sauté onions, zucchini and tomatoes in oil. Cook over low heat until tender, stirring occasionally. Pour into casserole dish and sprinkle with shredded cheese. Bake 30 minutes at 350°.

Summer Squash or Zucchini Casserole
Mary Olson

6 cups summer squash or zucchini, diced
1 cup carrots, shredded
$1/4$ cup onion, diced
8 oz. dry stuffing mix
$1/2$ cup margarine, melted
1 (10 oz.) can cream of mushroom soup
1 cup sour cream

Steam veggies 5 minutes until tender. Drain and set aside. Combine stuffing and melted margarine. Put half of stuffing mix in bottom of 9 x 13 pan. Mix vegetables, soup and sour cream and put over stuffing mix. Put remainder of stuffing mix on top. Bake 30 minutes uncovered at 350°.

Mashed Potato Casserole
Elizabeth O. Nice

4 large potatoes
$1/3$ cup sour cream or yogurt
pepper
$1/2$ tsp sugar
$1/4$ cup margarine
milk
2 cups spinach
$1/2$ cup Cheddar cheese

Cook and mash potatoes. Add sour cream or yogurt along with pepper, sugar and margarine. Add just enough milk to bring to proper consistency. Beat until fluffy. Add spinach. Place in greased casserole and top with cheese. Bake 20 minutes at 400°

Use more spinach, if you like. You can also stir additional cheese into the casserole mixture.

Quickie Casserole
Alicia Mortensen

2 cups shrimp, cooked
2 cups macaroni, cooked
$^1/_4$ cup onions, diced
$^1/_4$ cup Parmesan cheese
1 (10 oz.) can cream of chicken soup

$^1/_2$ cup milk
1 cup peas, cooked
salt and pepper to taste
2 cups saltines, crushed
$^1/_4$ cup margarine, melted

Mix all ingredients, except crackers and margarine, in 3-quart casserole.
Mix saltines with melted margarine and sprinkle on top. Bake 30 minutes
at 350°. (*Tuna or cooked chicken or can be used instead of shrimp.*)

Fish Casserole
Debbie Moody Bellows

1 lb. potatoes, thinly sliced
1 lb. firm white fish, cooked and flaked
$^1/_2$ cup onion, chopped
salt and pepper to taste

3 Tbsp flour
2 Tbsp margarine
2 cups milk

In a buttered casserole dish, layer potatoes, fish and onion; season with
salt and pepper. Combine melted margarine and flour in sauce pan. Stir in
milk and cook on medium until thickened. Pour sauce over layers in
casserole. Bake 1 hour at 350°, or until potatoes are soft.

(*Cheese, peas, mushrooms or sliced boiled eggs can be added to the layers.*)

Scallop Casserole
Sharon Moody

1 (12 oz.) box noodles, cooked and
   drained
6 Tbsp margarine
6 Tbsp flour
$^1/_2$ tsp salt
$^1/_8$ tsp pepper

4 cups milk
2 lbs. scallops, quartered and sautéed
2 (4 oz.) cans mushrooms, drained
$^1/_2$ cup cooking sherry
$^1/_2$ lb. grated sharp Cheddar cheese

Pour noodles into greased 4-quart casserole dish. In separate pan, melt margarine; blend in flour, salt and pepper. Cook over low heat until smooth.
Slowly add milk and cook until sauce thickens, stirring constantly. Add scallops, mushrooms and sherry to sauce. Pour over noodles, lifting with fork to
blend. Top with grated cheese. Cover and bake 45 to 50 minutes at 350°.

Mom's Tuna Casserole
Judy Moody Beck

1 (12 oz.) pkg. flat egg noodles
2 cups milk, or 1/2 evaporated and
   1/2 water
dash of pepper
2 (6 oz.) cans of tuna, drained

2 cans cream of mushroom soup
2 cups grated Cheddar cheese
2 eggs, hard-cooked and chopped
seasoned bread crumbs

Cook noodles, drain. Place noodles in large casserole dish and add remaining ingredients. Mix well. Top with bread crumbs. Bake uncovered at 350° for 30 minutes.

Tuna Mushroom Casserole
Peggy Jones

1 cup long-grain rice, uncooked
1 (10 oz.) can cream of mushroom soup
2 1/4 cups water
1/2 cup onion, chopped
1 (10 oz.) pkg. frozen peas

1 Tbsp Worcestershire sauce
1 (6 oz.) can tuna, drained and
   flaked
1 (4 oz.) can mushroom pieces,
   drained

Combine rice, soup, water, onion and Worcestershire sauce in large skillet. Stir well and bring to boil. Reduce heat, cover and cook over low heat about 25 minutes or until rice is tender. Stir occasionally. Fold in peas, tuna and mushroom pieces. Heat uncovered 5 minutes.

Tuna Wiggle
Bertha Moody

1 (10 oz.) can cream of mushroom soup
1 (6 oz.) can tuna, drained and flaked

1/2 cup peas, cooked
1 tsp Worcestershire sauce

Combine all ingredients and heat through. Serve over saltine crackers.

Vegetables

Broccoli Casserole
Dot Aho Moody

1 medium onion, chopped
$^1/_2$ stick margarine
1 can cream of chicken soup
$^1/_2$ cup milk

$^1/_4$ cup water
$^1/_2$ cup Cheez Whiz
1 (8 oz.) pkg. broccoli, cooked
1 cup minute rice, uncooked

Sauté onion in margarine until transparent. Add soup, water, milk and Cheez Whiz. Stir until smooth. Grease casserole dish, put rice and broccoli on bottom. Pour sauce over rice and broccoli and bake 40 to 50 minutes at 350°.

Creamed Cabbage
Marge Adams

1 small cabbage
2 tsp oil

3 Tbsp butter
$^1/_2$ cup cream

Cut cabbage into bite-size pieces. Bring pot of salted water to boil. Add oil to boiling water, then cook cabbage in water until tender. Drain, add butter and cream.

Sweet and Sour Red Cabbage
Carolyn Staples

1 red cabbage
1 cup water
1 cup cider vinegar
1 stick margarine

3 Tbsp salt
$1^1/_2$ cups sugar
1 cup applesauce

Shred cabbage and put in saucepan. Add water, vinegar, margarine, salt and sugar. Bring to a boil, then stir in applesauce. Simmer 1 hour.

Marinated Carrots
Judy Moody Beck

1 lb. carrots
1 large green pepper

2 medium onions
10 oz. French dressing

Peel and slice carrots into saucepan and boil until just tender. Drain and pour into a bowl. Chop peppers and onions and add to carrots. Mix in French dressing and refrigerate a few hours or overnight.

Corn Soufflé
Alice Wellman

1 Tbsp butter
2 Tbsp flour
1 cup milk
$^1/_2$ tsp salt

$^1/_2$ tsp pepper
1 (16 oz.) can creamed corn
2 eggs, separated

Melt butter, add flour and milk, and bring to a boil. Remove from heat and add salt and pepper. Stir in creamed corn and beaten egg yolks. Beat egg whites until stiff and fold into batter. Pour into buttered baking dish. Bake 35 to 40 minutes at 350°.

Company Green Beans
Clara Moody Kiener

$^1/_2$ lb. fresh mushrooms
2 Tbsp butter
garlic salt
lemon pepper

3 Tbsp white wine
1 (16 oz.) can green beans
sliced toasted almonds

Slice and sauté mushrooms in butter until tender. Season with salt and lemon pepper, add wine and simmer. Drain and rinse green beans twice in cold water, then add to mushrooms and cook about 45 minutes until liquid is almost gone. Sprinkle sliced almonds over beans and serve.

Pea Salad
Charlene Moody Ward

2 cans peas, or 1 (1 lb.) pkg.
  cooked frozen peas
1 small onion, chopped
4 oz. Cheddar cheese, cubed

2 eggs, hard-boiled and chopped
sweet pickle relish
mayonnaise
salt and pepper to taste

Combine all ingredients, adding just enough mayonnaise to moisten salad. Chill before serving.

Potato Pie
Gail Kennedy

1 lb. potatoes
1 medium onion
2 Tbsp oil
2 Tbsp margarine

1 clove chopped garlic
nutmeg
salt and pepper
1 cup grated Cheddar cheese

Wash potatoes and slice thinly, then dry thoroughly. Thinly slice onions and dice. Melt together margarine and oil in skillet and add onion. When onion is lightly cooked, add potatoes. While potatoes are cooking, add garlic and spices.

Once potatoes are cooked, use a spatula to shape them into a circle and press down, forming a loose patty. Cook a little longer, then flip and cook other side. Place patty in baking dish and cover with grated cheese. Broil until cheese melts and browns. Serve in wedges.

Oven-Fried Potatoes
Nancy Moody Genthner

4 large baking potatoes, unpeeled
$1/4$ cup vegetable oil
2 Tbsp Parmesan cheese
$1/4$ tsp garlic powder

$1/4$ tsp paprika
$1/8$ tsp pepper
$1/2$ tsp salt

Wash unpeeled potatoes and cut lengthwise into wedges. Place skin-side down in 13 x 9 inch baking pan. Combine remaining ingredients; brush over potatoes. Bake at 375° for 1 hour, brushing with oil/cheese mixture at 15 minute intervals. Turn potatoes over last 15 minutes.

Twice-Baked Potatoes
Cathy Hopler

6 large baking potatoes
$^1/_2$ cup butter or margarine, softened
$^3/_4$ to 1 cup milk
3 Tbsp onions, minced
1 Tbsp chives, snipped

$^1/_2$ tsp salt
dash pepper
1$^1/_2$ cups shredded Cheddar cheese
paprika
bacon bits (optional)

Bake potatoes at 400° for 60 minutes or until soft. Cut a lengthwise slice from the top of the potatoes. Scoop out the pulp and place in a bowl. Mash pulp with butter. Blend in milk, onion, chives, salt, pepper and 1 cup of the cheese. Refill potato shells. Top with remaining cheese and sprinkle with paprika. May also sprinkle with bacon bits if desired. Bake at 375° for 25 to 30 minutes or until heated through.

Scalloped Onions with Cheese Sauce
Faye E. Moody

4 to 6 medium onions
$^1/_4$ cup margarine
$^1/_4$ cup flour

2 cups milk
$^1/_2$ tsp salt
2 cups grated sharp
    Cheddar cheese

Thinly slice onions and place in 1$^1/_2$-quart casserole dish. Melt margarine in skillet and blend in flour. Add milk and cook over low heat until thickened, stirring constantly. Add salt and grated cheese, stir until cheese melts. Pour sauce over onions and bake 1 hour at 350°.

Spinach Casserole
Thelma Moody

1 pkg. spinach, cooked and chopped
1 Tbsp grated onion
$^3/_4$ cup grated sharp Cheddar cheese
1 egg, beaten

1 (10 oz.) can mushroom soup
1 cup stuffing mix
$^1/_2$ cup margarine

Combine all ingredients and mix well. Pour in greased casserole dish and bake 30 minutes at 350°.

Rose's Baked Beans
Nancy Moody Genthner

2 cups beans (yellow eye or pea)
1 small onion, quartered
$^1/_2$ cup brown sugar
$^1/_2$ cup molasses
$^1/_2$ tsp salt

dash of pepper
1 tsp prepared mustard
$^1/_2$ tsp ginger
2 Tbsp shortening, or a piece of
  salt pork

Cover beans with water and soak overnight. Place onion in bottom of bean pot. Drain beans and place in pot. Mix brown sugar, molasses, salt, pepper, mustard and ginger with a little hot water and pour over beans. Add enough hot water to cover beans. Put shortening or salt pork on top. Cover pot and bake 6 hours at 325°. Check often, adding hot water as needed. Cover of pot may be removed for last hour.

Desserts

Bread Pudding
Jean Moody

4 slices bread, cubed
3 cups milk
1 egg, beaten
$^1/_2$ cup seedless raisins

$^3/_4$ cup sugar
$^1/_4$ tsp salt
$^1/_2$ tsp nutmeg

In saucepan, heat bread in half of the milk. When hot, add remaining milk, then add other ingredients. Pour into casserole dish and bake 1 hour at 350°, stirring occasionally.

Mom's Gingerbread
Bertha Moody

1 egg
$^1/_2$ cup sugar
$^1/_4$ cup molasses
$^1/_4$ cup shortening, melted
1 cup flour

1 tsp baking soda
$^1/_2$ tsp salt
1 tsp ginger
$^1/_2$ cup boiling water

Mix together egg and sugar, then add molasses and shortening. Mix well. Stir in dry ingredients and then the hot water. Pour batter into greased and floured 8-inch pan. Bake 30 minutes at 350°. Serve hot with whipped cream.

Gingerbread
Sharon Moody

$^1/_2$ cup shortening
$^1/_2$ cup sugar
1 egg
1 cup molasses
$2^1/_2$ cups flour
$1^1/_2$ tsp baking soda

1 tsp cinnamon
$^3/_4$ tsp ginger
$^1/_2$ tsp cloves
$^1/_2$ tsp salt
1 cup hot water

Mix shortening, sugar, egg and molasses and beat well. Sift together dry ingredients and add to mixture. Stir in hot water. Pour into 9 x 13 inch pan and bake 45 to 50 minutes at 350°.

Indian Pudding
Cynthia Hilton

5 Tbsp cornmeal
1 quart milk
2 Tbsp margarine
$^3/_4$ cup molasses
1 tsp salt

$^3/_4$ tsp cinnamon
$^1/_2$ tsp ginger
2 eggs, well-beaten
1 cup evaporated milk

Scald the milk with the cornmeal added, then mix in margarine, molasses, salt, spices and eggs. Pour into a well-greased dish, add the evaporated milk but do not stir. Bake 1 hour at 350°. Serve warm with a scoop of ice cream.

Blueberry Crisp
Andrea Moody Newbert

2 cups blueberries
1 cup oatmeal
$^1/_3$ cup flour
$^1/_2$ cup brown sugar

$^1/_2$ tsp salt
1 tsp cinnamon
$^1/_3$ cup margarine, softened

Pour blueberries into 8-inch casserole dish. In a separate bowl, combine and mix other ingredients until crumbly, then sprinkle over blueberries. Bake 35 to 40 minutes at 350°. Serve warm topped with whipped cream or ice cream.

Cherry Blossom Dessert
Nancy Moody Genthner

$^1/_4$ cup flour
1 can sour cherries, drained (save
  $^3/_4$ cup of the juice)

1 cup sugar
$^1/_4$ tsp red food coloring
$^1/_4$ tsp almond extract

Combine ingredients, except cherries, in sauce pan and cook over medium heat until thickened. Add cherries. Set aside to cool while you prepare the oatmeal crumb crust (next page).

Crust:

1½ cups flour
1 tsp salt
½ tsp baking soda

1 cup packed brown sugar
1 cup quick-cooking oatmeal
½ cup shortening

Sift flour, salt and baking soda. Blend in brown sugar and oatmeal and cut in shortening. Press half the oatmeal crumbs into ungreased 8-inch pan. Spread with cooled cherry filling and cover with the remaining oatmeal crumbs. Bake 25 to 30 minutes at 350°. Top with whipped cream or ice cream.

Apple Pudding
Bertha Moody

3 cups flour, sifted
½ cup sugar
3 tsp baking powder
1 tsp salt

3 Tbsp shortening
1½ cups milk
6 apples, peeled and sliced
cinnamon sugar

Sift together flour, sugar, baking powder and salt. Cut in shortening and stir in milk. Fold in sliced apples. Pour in greased 9-inch baking pan, sprinkle the top with cinnamon sugar. Bake 45 minutes at 375°.

Sauce:

2 Tbsp margarine
2 heaping Tbsp cornstarch
1 cup sugar

2 cups water
1 tsp vanilla

Melt margarine in water in large saucepan. Combine cornstarch and sugar in small bowl, add a little cold water to form a smooth paste. Stir into hot water and bring to a boil, stirring a few minutes until slightly thickened. Remove from heat and add 1 tsp vanilla. Serve over pudding.

Banana Dessert
Nancy Moody Genthner

Crust:

½ cup butter, softened

1 cup flour

Mix together and press into 13 x 9 inch baking dish. Bake at 350° for 8 minutes.

Filling:

1 (8 oz.) pkg.cream cheese, softened
1 cup confectioner's sugar
1 (12 oz.) container Cool Whip
4 bananas

2 (3 oz.) pkg. banana instant
    pudding
3 cups milk

Combine softened cream cheese and 1 cup confectioner's sugar. Spread over cooled crust. Spread half of Cool Whip over cream cheese mixture. Slice bananas over Cool Whip. Mix instant banana pudding with milk. Spread over bananas. Cover with remaining Cool Whip. Refrigerate until serving.

Grapefruit Baked Alaska
Brian Moody

3 egg whites
$^1/_4$ tsp cream of tartar
6 Tbsp sugar

2 grapefruits
vanilla ice cream

Beat egg whites with cream of tartar until soft peaks form. Gradually beat in sugar until egg whites are stiff and glossy. Cut grapefruits in half and section them. Place scoop of ice cream on each grapefruit and carefully cover with whipped egg white meringue. Brown quickly in 450° oven. Serve immediately.

Strawberry Rhubarb Puff
Debbie Moody Bellows

3 cups rhubarb, chopped
1 quart strawberries, sliced
$1^1/_2$ cups sugar, or $^3/_4$ cup honey
2 cups flour
2 Tbsp sugar
butter

3 tsp baking powder
1 tsp salt
$^1/_3$ cup oil
$^2/_3$ cup milk
2 Tbsp sugar
1 tsp cinnamon

Mix together rhubarb, strawberries and $1^1/_2$ cups sugar. Place in ungreased 9-inch pan. Place in 350° oven until hot. Mix flour, 1 Tbsp sugar, baking powder and salt in bowl. Pour oil and milk into measuring cup—DON'T MIX—and stir into flour. Stir until dough cleans sides of bowl and forms into a ball. Drop dough by spoonfuls onto hot fruit. Make an indentation in each drop of dough and dot with butter. Mix 2 Tbsp sugar with cinnamon and sprinkle over dough. Return to oven and bake 20 to 25 minutes. Serve warm.

Rhubarb Dessert
Jean Moody

1 cup flour
5 Tbsp powdered sugar
$^1/_2$ cup margarine
2 eggs
$1^1/_2$ cups sugar

$^1/_4$ cup flour
$^3/_4$ tsp baking powder
2 cups rhubarb, chopped
1 tsp vanilla

Mix 1 cup flour, powdered sugar and margarine together to consistency of pie crust dough. Pat into 9-inch baking pan. Bake 15 minutes at 350° until crust is golden brown. Beat eggs, add sugar and mix thoroughly, then add remaining ingredients. Pour over crust and bake 30 minutes at 350°.

Eggless Chocolate Pudding
Alice Wellman

$^2/_3$ cup sugar
$^1/_4$ cup cornstarch
$^1/_8$ tsp salt
3 Tbsp cocoa

$2^3/_4$ cups milk
2 Tbsp margarine
1 tsp vanilla

Mix together sugar, cornstarch, salt and cocoa. Gradually add milk and pour into saucepan. Bring to boil over medium heat, stirring constantly. Boil 1 minute and remove from heat. Stir in margarine and vanilla. Chill and serve.

For Eggless Vanilla Pudding, omit the cocoa and $^1/_3$ cup of the sugar.

Mom's Chocolate Pudding
Judy Moody Beck

1 (12 oz.) can evaporated milk
$1^1/_2$ cups water
1 cup sugar
2 rounded Tbsp cornstarch

4 level Tbsp cocoa
$^1/_2$ tsp salt
1 tsp vanilla

Heat evaporated milk and water in double boiler. Mix together sugar, cornstarch, cocoa and salt. Add 3 to 4 Tbsp hot milk to the dry ingredients and stir until smooth. Add cocoa mixture to heated milk and cook, stirring until thickened. Cool, then add vanilla. Serve with whipped cream.

Chocolate Torte
Jan Jones

1 stick margarine
1 cup flour
$^1/_2$ cup chopped nuts
8 oz. cream cheese
1 cup powdered sugar

12 oz. Cool Whip
3 cups cold milk
2 pkgs.(3 oz.) instant chocolate
    pudding mix

Mix margarine, flour and nuts and pat into 13 x 9 inch pan. Bake 15 minutes at 350°. Cool. Beat together cream cheese and sugar. Add $^1/_2$ of Cool Whip and spread over crust. Beat pudding mix with milk and spread over cream cheese. Top with remaining Cool Whip and decorate with chopped nuts. Refrigerate until served.

Eclair Torte
Nancy Moody Genthner

1 cup water
$^1/_2$ cup butter (no substitutes)
$^1/_4$ tsp salt
1 cup flour
4 eggs

1 (8 oz.) pkg. cream cheese, softened
2 (3 oz.)pkgs. instant vanilla pudding
3 cups cold milk
1 (12 oz.) carton Cool Whip
chocolate syrup

In saucepan over medium heat, bring water, butter and salt to a boil. Add flour all at once, stir until a smooth ball forms. Remove from heat and let stand for 5 minutes. Add eggs, one at a time, beating well with a wooden spoon after each addition. Beat until smooth. Spread into a greased 13 x 9 inch baking pan. Bake at 400° for 30 to 35 minutes, or until puffed and golden brown. Cool completely on a wire rack. If desired, remove puff from pan and place on a serving platter.

In a mixing bowl, beat cream cheese, pudding mix and milk until smooth. Spread over puff. Refrigerate for 20 minutes. Spread with whipped topping and refrigerate again. Drizzle with chocolate syrup just before serving. Refrigerate leftovers. Makes 12 servings.

Refrigerator Pie
Jean Moody

1¹/₂ cups flour
³/₄ cup margarine
³/₄ cup chopped pecans or walnuts
8 oz. cream cheese

1 cup powdered sugar
2 cups Cool Whip
2 (3 oz.) pkgs. instant lemon pudding
3 cups milk

Blend flour, margarine and chopped nuts. Press into a 13 x 9 pan. Bake 10 to 15 minutes at 350° and let cool. Beat cream cheese and powdered sugar and blend in 1 cup Cool Whip. Spread over cooled crust. Combine pudding and milk and mix until thickened. Spread over cream cheese and spread with remaining Cool Whip. Refrigerate.

Gillie Whoppers
Naomi Walker

¹/₂ cup margarine
³/₄ cup sugar
2 eggs
³/₄ cup flour, sifted
¹/₄ tsp baking powder

¹/₄ tsp salt
2 Tbsp cocoa
1 tsp vanilla
¹/₂ cup chopped nuts
1 pkg. miniature marshmallows

Cream margarine and sugar. Add eggs, one at a time, beating after each addition. Add sifted dry ingredients and stir well. Add vanilla and chopped nuts. Pour batter into greased 9-inch pan and bake 25 minutes at 350°. Remove from oven and sprinkle marshmallows on top, keeping away from edges. Return to oven for 2 minutes. Remove from oven and frost.

Frosting:

¹/₂ cup light brown sugar
¹/₄ cup water
2 squares unsweetened chocolate

3 Tbsp margarine
1 tsp vanilla
1¹/₂ cups powdered sugar

Combine brown sugar, water and chocolate and boil 3 minutes. Add remaining ingredients, mix and spread over marshmallows. Cool and cut in squares.

Pumpkin Cake Roll
Anne Braley

3 eggs
1 cup sugar
2/3 cup pumpkin
1 tsp lemon juice
3/4 cup flour
1 tsp baking powder
2 tsp cinnamon

1 tsp ginger
1/2 tsp salt
1 cup powdered sugar
2 (3 oz.) pkgs. cream cheese
4 Tbsp margarine
1/2 tsp vanilla
1/2 cup chopped nuts

Beat eggs with electric mixer on high for 5 minutes. Gradually add sugar, stir in pumpkin and add lemon juice. In a separate bowl, stir together flour, baking powder, cinnamon, ginger and salt. Fold dry ingredients into pumpkin and spread into greased and floured 15 x 10 inch pan. Bake 15 minutes at 375°.

Turn cake onto a towel sprinkled with powdered sugar. Roll cake and towel together and let cool. Beat together powdered sugar, cream cheese, margarine and vanilla. Beat until smooth. Carefully unroll cake and spread with cream cheese and nuts. Roll and chill. Sprinkle with powdered sugar and serve.

# Pies

Mom's Pie Crust
Bertha Moody

1 heaping cup shortening
3 cups flour

1 tsp salt
³/4 cup cold water

Cut shortening into flour and salt until the mixture resembles coarse cornmeal. Add water, a little at a time, until the dough just holds together. Adding too much water will make the dough tough. Roll out dough on floured surface. Makes two double-crust pies.

No-Fail Pie Crust
Pat Caldwell

1 egg, beaten
1 Tbsp vinegar
1 lb. lard or Crisco

5 cups flour
dash of salt

Combine egg and vinegar in measuring cup and add enough cold water to equal 1 cup liquid. In large bowl, cut shortening into flour and salt. Add water, egg and vinegar mixture and mix until dough is moist. This dough freezes well. Makes 4 double-crust pies.

Meringue
Thelma Kennedy

2 egg whites
3 Tbsp cold water
1 tsp baking powder

6 Tbsp granulated sugar
dash of salt

Combine egg whites, cold water and baking powder and beat until stiff. Continue to beat and gradually add sugar and salt. Spread meringue on pie. Bake in preheated 425° oven. Remove after a few minutes, when meringue starts to brown.

Fresh Rhubarb Pie
Bertha Moody

2 cups rhubarb, chopped
2 eggs
1 cup sugar

1 Tbsp tapioca
1 tsp salt
1/3 tsp nutmeg

Place chopped rhubarb in saucepan and cover with water. Bring water to steaming and immediately drain rhubarb. Beat eggs; add sugar, tapioca, salt and nutmeg. Add rhubarb and pour batter into unbaked 9-inch pie shell. Cover with top crust and pinch crusts together. Bake 45 minutes at 350°.

This may be made without "steaming" the rhubarb. Mom always steamed it first, because she thought it removed some of the sour taste and made a more custard-type pie.

Rhubarb-Orange Cream Pie
Ona Moody

$^1/_4$ cup margarine, softened
3 Tbsp orange juice
3 eggs, separated
$1^1/_4$ cups sugar

$^1/_4$ cup flour
$^1/_4$ tsp salt
$2^1/_2$ cups rhubarb, chopped
$^1/_3$ cup pecans

Combine margarine and orange juice with egg yolks and beat thoroughly. Add 1 cup sugar, flour and salt, beat well. Add rhubarb and stir. Add remaining sugar to egg whites and beat until stiff. Fold beaten egg whites into rhubarb batter and pour into unbaked 9-inch pie shell. Sprinkle with nuts. Bake 15 minutes on bottom rack of 375° oven, then reduce heat to 350° and bake 40 to 45 minutes longer.

Apple Cranberry-Raisin Pie
Jan Jones

5 large apples, thinly sliced
1 cup cranberries
$^3/_4$ cup sugar
$^1/_2$ cup raisins, diced

2 Tbsp margarine
3 Tbsp flour
$1^1/_2$ tsp lemon peel, or dash of
    lemon juice

Toss together all ingredients to coat well. Pour into unbaked 9-inch pie shell and cover with top crust. Cut vents in top crust. Bake 10 minutes at 450°, then reduce heat to 350° and bake 30 to 40 minutes longer.

Butter Pie
Bertha Moody

2 eggs
²/₃ cup sugar
2 Tbsp flour
¹/₄ tsp salt

2 Tbsp butter, melted
1 tsp vanilla
1³/₄ cups milk

Beat eggs in large bowl. In separate bowl, combine sugar, flour and salt and add to eggs. Mix well. Add melted butter, vanilla and milk. Mix thoroughly. Pour into unbaked 9-inch pie shell. Bake 15 minutes at 400°, then reduce heat to 300° and cook 25 to 30 minutes longer.

Pumpkin Pie I
Laura Jones

5 eggs, well beaten
1¹/₂ cups sugar
1¹/₂ tsp cinnamon
¹/₂ tsp cloves

1 tsp nutmeg
1 tsp salt
2 cups pumpkin, cooked
1 (12 oz.) can evaporated milk

Mix together eggs, sugar, spices and salt. Beat well. Add pumpkin and milk. Stir well and pour batter into unbaked 9-inch pie shell. Bake 15 minutes at 400°, then reduce heat to 325° and cook 45 to 60 minutes longer. Pie is done when a knife inserted in the center comes out clean.

Pumpkin Pie II
Jean Moody

1 cup sugar
1 Tbsp cornstarch
¹/₂ tsp salt
¹/₂ tsp cinnamon
¹/₂ tsp ground ginger
¹/₂ tsp ground nutmeg

1³/₄ cups pumpkin, cooked
2 eggs, beaten
1¹/₂ Tbsp margarine, melted
¹/₈ cup molasses
1¹/₂ cups milk

Sift together sugar, cornstarch, salt, cinnamon, ginger and nutmeg. Stir in pumpkin. Add eggs, margarine, molasses and milk. Pour batter into unbaked 9-inch pie shell. Bake 15 minutes at 400°, then reduce heat to 350° and bake 50 minutes.

Peanut Butter Pie
Judy Moody Beck

1 (8 oz.) pkg. cream cheese, softened   1 (12 oz.) Cool Whip
¹/₂ cup chunky peanut butter   1 chocolate cookie crust
1 cup powdered sugar

Cream together peanut butter, cream cheese and sugar. Fold in Cool
Whip and pour batter into chocolate cookie crust (available at stores, or
make your own). Refrigerate until serving, or freeze and serve frozen. Top
with hot fudge and whipped cream.

Lemon Sponge Pie
Ona Moody

¹/₃ cup lemon juice and grated rind   3 heaping Tbsp flour
1¹/₂ cups sugar   3 eggs, separated
1 Tbsp margarine, melted   1¹/₂ cups milk

Beat together juice, sugar, margarine, flour and egg yolks. Add milk and
stir. Beat egg whites until stiff and fold into batter. Pour into unbaked
9-inch pie shell and bake 30 minutes at 350°.

Little Pecan Pies
Dorothy Bruns Moody

¹/₂ lb. butter   2 eggs
6 oz. cream cheese, softened   1¹/₂ cups brown sugar
2 cups flour   2 Tbsp margarine, melted
1 cup chopped pecans   dash of salt
¹/₂ Tbsp vanilla

Using pastry blender, mix together cream cheese, flour and butter until
well blended. Press 1-inch balls of pastry into miniature cupcake tins,
forming crusts. Combine and blend together remaining ingredients for
filling. Fill cupcake tins half full. Bake 15 minutes at 350°, reduce heat to
250° and cook 10 minutes longer.

Old-Fashioned Cream Pie
Bertha Moody

3 cups flour
1¹/₃ cups shortening
1 tsp baking soda
2 tsp cream of tartar

¹/₂ tsp salt
1 Tbsp sugar
³/₄ cup milk

Cut shortening into dry ingredients and add milk; mix well. Divide into 4. Roll out each piece of dough and place on shallow, 10-inch ironstone plate. Trim edges. Bake dough about 10 minutes at 400°, until lightly browned. Slide crust onto rack to cool.

Cream Filling:

1 cup sugar
¹/₂ cup flour
¹/₂ tsp salt

1 egg
2 cups milk
1 tsp vanilla

Combine sugar, flour and salt with beaten egg. Heat milk in double boiler. Once hot, add ¹/₄ cup of hot milk to egg mixture. Mix well and stir into remaining hot milk. Stir until thickened. Remove from heat and add vanilla. Cool filling. To assemble pie, place one crust on plate and cover with ¹/₂ the cream filling. Top with second crust. Makes 2 pies.

This was one of our favorite desserts as children.

Cakes

Fresh Apple Cake
Marge Adams

2 or 3 medium apples
1 cup sugar
$^1/_2$ cup margarine, melted
1 egg
$1^1/_2$ cups flour
1 tsp cinnamon

$^1/_2$ tsp nutmeg
$^1/_2$ tsp allspice
1 tsp baking soda
$^1/_2$ tsp salt
$^1/_2$ cup raisins
$^1/_2$ cup chopped nuts

Peel and chop apples and place in large bowl; add sugar and let stand 10 minutes. Blend melted margarine and unbeaten egg into apples. Sift flour, spices, soda and salt, and stir into batter. Fold in raisins and nuts. Pour into greased 8-inch pan and bake 40 to 45 minutes at 350°. Cool cake in pan 10 minutes before removing. Top with whipped cream if desired.

Melt-in-Your-Mouth Blueberry Cake
Margaret Moody Wellman

4 eggs, separated
2 cups sugar
3 cups blueberries
3 cups flour
1 cup shortening

$^1/_2$ tsp salt
2 tsp vanilla
2 tsp baking powder
$^2/_3$ cup milk

Beat egg whites until stiff, then fold in $^1/_2$ cup sugar and set aside. Dust blueberries with 1 Tbsp flour and set aside. Cream shortening, add salt, vanilla and remaining sugar. Add egg yolks and beat until creamy. Sift dry ingredients and add to batter alternately with milk. Fold in beaten egg whites and blueberries. Turn batter into well-greased 9 x 13 inch pan and sprinkle with sugar. Bake 55 minutes at 350°.

Carrot Cake
Brian Moody

2 cups flour	1 cup honey, or 2 cups sugar
$^1/_2$ tsp salt	$1^1/_4$ cup oil
2 tsp nutmeg	4 eggs
2 tsp cinnamon	3 cups carrots, grated
1 tsp baking powder	1 cup combined nuts & raisins (optional)

Combine dry ingredients, and add honey (or sugar) and oil. Add eggs one at a time, mixing well each time. Stir in carrots, nuts and raisins. Pour batter into a greased and floured 9 x 13 inch pan. Bake 30 to 40 minutes at 350°, or until cake tester comes out clean. Cool and frost with Cream Cheese Frosting.

Cream Cheese Frosting:

Cream together one stick of softened margarine with 1 pkg. (8 oz.) softened cream cheese. Beat in either honey to taste or 1 lb. powdered sugar. Use your imagination for flavorings: rum, almond or vanilla extracts, orange peel, or nuts.

Carrot Cake II
Laura Jones

1 cup oil	2 tsp baking powder
2 cups sugar	2 tsp baking soda
4 eggs	1 tsp cinnamon
3 cups grated carrots	1 tsp vanilla
2 cups flour	1 cup chopped nuts, optional

Mix together oil and sugar, add eggs and carrots and mix well. Add dry ingredients and mix thoroughly. Add vanilla and nuts. Pour batter into a greased and floured 9 x 13 inch pan and bake 1 hour, 10 minutes, at 300°.

Cream Cheese Frosting:

3 oz. cream cheese, softened	1 tsp vanilla
$^1/_4$ cup margarine, softened	powdered sugar
1 tsp instant coffee	

Cream margarine and cream cheese, beat in coffee and vanilla. Add enough powdered sugar to make frosting thick enough to spread, and frost cake while still hot.

Zucchini Carrot Cake
Nellie Moody Jones

2 eggs
1 cup sugar
²/₃ cup oil
1¹/₄ cups flour
1 tsp baking powder
1 tsp baking soda

1 tsp cinnamon
¹/₂ tsp salt
1 cup carrots, grated
1 cup zucchini, grated
¹/₂ cup chopped nuts

Beat together eggs and sugar, add oil and beat well. Add sifted dry ingredients and beat with electric mixer 3 minutes at High speed. Stir in carrots, zucchini and nuts. Pour into greased 9-inch pan and bake 35 minutes at 350°. Frost with Cream Cheese Frosting (p. 140).

Auntie's One-Egg Cake
Brian Moody

1¹/₄ cups plus 2 Tbsp flour
1 cup sugar
2 tsp baking powder
¹/₂ tsp salt

¹/₃ cup shortening
²/₃ cup milk
1 tsp vanilla
1 egg

Combine dry ingredients. Add shortening, milk and vanilla, and beat 2 minutes on Medium speed. Add egg and beat 2 minutes more. Bake 35 to 40 minutes at 350° in a greased and floured 8-inch pan. Top with New England Nutmeg Sauce.

New England Nutmeg Sauce:

1 cup sugar
2 Tbsp flour
dash of salt

2 cups boiling water
1 Tbsp margarine
1 tsp nutmeg or cinnamon

Combine sugar, flour and salt. Gradually add boiling water, stirring constantly. Pour into double boiler, add margarine and cook 5 minutes or until thickened. Remove from heat and stir in nutmeg. Serve over cake.

Hot Milk Cake
Arletta Flagg

2 eggs
1 cup sugar
1 cup flour
1 tsp baking powder

$^1/_2$ cup hot milk
3 Tbsp margarine
1 tsp vanilla

Beat eggs until light. Slowly add sugar and beat. Fold sifted dry ingredients into egg and sugar mixture. Heat milk until it starts to steam, *but do not boil.* Add margarine to hot milk and mix into batter. Add vanilla. Bake in greased and floured 8-inch pan for 30 minutes at 350°. Frost or top with Mom's Chocolate Sauce.

Mom's Chocolate Sauce
Debbie Moody Bellows

$^1/_2$ cup sugar
1 Tbsp cocoa
1 Tbsp cornstarch

pinch of salt
1 cup hot water

Combine dry ingredients and mix with a little cold water until smooth. Bring 1 cup water to a boil. Add cocoa mixture and cook until slightly thickened.

(Served hot over a piece of yellow cake or cupcake, this was a favorite dessert at our house.)

Elizabeth's Cake
Rebecca Little

1 (18 oz.) box yellow cake mix
1 cup vanilla pudding, cooked
1 (20 oz.) can crushed pineapple,
    drained

1 (12 oz.) container Cool Whip
1 cup shredded coconut
$^1/_2$ cup crushed nuts
$^1/_2$ cup maraschino cherries,
    chopped

Bake cake mix in 9 x 13 inch pan, according to package directions. Cool, then spread pudding over cake. Spread pineapple over pudding and top with Cool Whip. Sprinkle Cool Whip with coconut, nuts and cherries.

Mocha Cake
Arletta Flagg

4 Tbsp margarine
1 cup sugar
1 tsp baking soda
1 cup buttermilk, or sour milk

1¹/₂ cups flour
¹/₂ cup cocoa
¹/₄ cup strong coffee
1 tsp vanilla

Cream together margarine and sugar. Stir baking soda into milk and add to creamed ingredients. Sift flour and cocoa and stir into batter, then mix in coffee and vanilla. Pour batter into a greased and floured 9-inch-square pan. Bake 35 to 40 minutes at 350°.

Kaye's Pound Cake
Rebecca Little

5 eggs
3 cups sugar
¹/₂ cup margarine
¹/₂ cup shortening
3 cups flour

¹/₂ tsp salt
¹/₂ tsp baking powder
1 cup milk
1 tsp lemon flavoring

Combine eggs, sugar, margarine and shortening, and beat until light and fluffy. Add sifted dry ingredients to batter alternately with milk and lemon. Pour into greased and floured angel food cake pan and bake 1 hour at 350°.

Chocolate Cake
Jean Moody

1 cup margarine
1 cup hot water
¹/₂ cup cocoa
1 tsp baking soda
¹/₂ cup buttermilk

2 cups sugar
2 cups flour
2 eggs, lightly beaten
1 tsp vanilla

Combine margarine, hot water and cocoa in saucepan and bring to a boil. Stir baking soda into buttermilk and set aside. Mix sugar and flour in large bowl and pour in heated ingredients. Beat well. Add eggs, vanilla and buttermilk/baking soda, and mix until smooth. Pour batter into a greased and floured 10 x 15 inch pan. Bake 20 minutes at 400°. Cool and then cover with Chocolate Frosting (next page).

Chocolate Frosting:

6 Tbsp margarine   1¹/₂ cups sugar
6 Tbsp milk   1 cup chocolate chips

Combine margarine, milk and sugar in a saucepan and boil rapidly for 30 seconds. Add chocolate chips and stir until frosting is smooth. Pour hot frosting over cake.

Filigree Devil's Food Cake
Marion Whitmore

1¹/₂ cups sifted flour   1 tsp salt
1¹/₄ cups sugar   ²/₃ cup shortening
¹/₂ cup cocoa   1 cup milk
1¹/₄ tsp baking soda   1 tsp vanilla
¹/₄ tsp cream of tartar   2 eggs

Sift dry ingredients into mixer bowl. Drop in shortening, add ²/₃ cup of the milk and vanilla and beat 2 minutes on medium speed. Scrape bowl continuously while mixing. Add eggs and remaining milk and beat 2 minutes longer. Pour batter into 2 deep, 8-inch round pans (greased and floured) and bake 30 to 40 minutes at 350°. Frost with favorite frosting.

Crazy Chocolate Cake
Brian Moody

3 cups flour   1 tsp salt
2 cups sugar   ³/₄ cup oil
6 Tbsp cocoa   2 Tbsp vinegar
2 tsp baking soda   2 tsp vanilla
2 cups water

Combine all ingredients and beat well. Pour batter into greased and floured 9 x 13 inch pan and bake 40 minutes at 350°. Frost with fluffy Cocoa Frosting.

Fluffy Cocoa Frosting:

³/₄ cup cocoa   ¹/₂ cup margarine
4 cups powdered sugar   1 tsp vanilla
1 tsp instant coffee   ¹/₂ cup evaporated milk

Mix cocoa, sugar and coffee. Reserve one-third and cream the remainder together with the margarine. Blend in vanilla and half the milk. Add remaining cocoa-coffee mixture and blend well. Add remaining milk to batter and beat to desired consistency.

This same Crazy Cake recipe was contributed by Kathy Kinney. She bakes it in a greased bundt pan at 350° for 45 minutes and frosts it with the following:

Whoopie Frosting:

Mix together $^1/_2$ cup Crisco, 1 box confectioner's sugar, 8 Tbsp Marshmallow Fluff and milk. Put first 3 ingredients in mixing bowl and add milk slowly, beating until fluffy.

Wowie Chocolate Cake
Nancy Moody Genthner

1 cup sugar	$^1/_3$ cup oil
$1^1/_2$ cups flour	1 tsp vanilla
$^1/_2$ tsp salt	1 cup cold water
$^1/_4$ cup cocoa	1 Tbsp vinegar
1 tsp baking soda	

Sift dry ingredients into bowl. Add the liquid ingredients and stir until smooth, beat 2 minutes. Pour into ungreased 8-inch-square pan and bake for 35 minutes at 350°.

A nice moist cake for a small family.

Pistachio Nut Cake
Betty Dyer

1 box yellow cake mix	4 eggs
1 box pistachio pudding mix	$^1/_2$ cup oil
$^1/_2$ cup orange juice	$^3/_4$ cup chocolate syrup
$^1/_2$ cup water	

Combine mixes, orange juice, water, eggs and oil in mixing bowl. Beat with electric mixer 2 minutes on medium speed, until smooth. Pour $^3/_4$ of batter into a greased and floured tube pan. Add chocolate syrup to remaining batter and pour over batter in pan. Bake 1 hour at 350°.

Lazy Daisy Oatmeal Cake
Susan Moody

1 cup dry oatmeal
$^1/_4$ cup boiling water
$^1/_2$ cup margarine
1 cup packed brown sugar
1 cup sugar
1 tsp vanilla

2 eggs
$1^1/_2$ cups flour
1 tsp baking soda
$^3/_4$ tsp cinnamon
$^1/_4$ tsp nutmeg
dash of salt

Combine oatmeal and boiling water in small bowl and set aside for 20 minutes. Beat together margarine, sugars, vanilla and eggs. Add dry ingredients, then the oatmeal. Pour batter into greased and floured 9 x 13 inch pan and bake 35 to 40 minutes at 350°.

Frosting:

$^1/_4$ cup margarine
$^1/_2$ cup brown sugar
3 Tbsp water

$^1/_3$ cup chopped nuts
$^3/_4$ cup coconut

Combine margarine, sugar and water in saucepan and heat until melted. Add nuts and coconut, mix well and pour over cooled cake.

Snackin' Cake
Nancy Moody Genthner

$1^2/_3$ cups flour
1 cup brown sugar
1 tsp baking soda
$^1/_2$ tsp salt
$^3/_4$ cup dry oatmeal
1 tsp allspice

2 Tbsp molasses
1 cup water
$^1/_3$ cup oil
1 tsp vinegar
$^1/_2$ cup raisins

Mix together dry ingredients. In large bowl, combine molasses, water, oil and vinegar. Mix in dry ingredients and raisins. Pour batter in greased and floured 8-inch-square pan and bake 35 to 40 minutes at 350°.

Tomato Soup Cake
Doris Moody Eaton

1 cup sugar
$^1/_2$ cup shortening
1 tsp baking soda
1 (12 oz.) can tomato soup
2 cups flour
2 tsp baking powder

1 tsp cinnamon
1 tsp cloves
1 tsp nutmeg
1 tsp salt
1 cup seeded raisins
$^1/_2$ cup chopped walnuts

Beat together sugar, shortening and baking soda. Add tomato soup and mix well. Sift dry ingredients and add to batter. Mix well. Stir in raisins and nuts. Pour batter into greased and floured 9 x 13 inch pan. Bake 45 minutes at 350°, or until toothpick inserted in center of cake comes out clean.

Cookies

Mom's Fat Molasses Cookies

Nancy Moody Genthner

$^1/_2$ cup sugar
$^1/_2$ cup shortening
$^1/_2$ cup buttermilk or sour milk
$^1/_2$ cup molasses
$2^1/_4$ cups flour

$^1/_2$ tsp salt
$^1/_2$ tsp cinnamon
$^1/_2$ tsp ginger
1 rounded tsp baking soda

Cream together sugar and shortening. Add sour milk and molasses and mix well. Stir in dry ingredients. Let dough set in refrigerator for 30 minutes. Roll out to $^1/_2$-inch thick and cut with round cookie cutter. Place on ungreased baking pan and sprinkle with sugar. Bake 15 to 20 minutes at 350°.

Thick Molasses Cookies

Nellie Moody Jones

1 egg
$^1/_2$ cup sugar
$^1/_4$ cup shortening
$^2/_3$ cup molasses
$^1/_2$ cup buttermilk or sour milk
1 tsp baking soda

$^1/_2$ tsp salt
$^1/_4$ tsp cloves
1 tsp cinnamon
$^1/_2$ tsp ginger
2 tsp baking powder
$2^1/_2$ cups flour

Cream egg, sugar and shortening; add molasses and mix well. Dissolve baking soda in buttermilk and stir into mixture. Add sifted dry ingredients. Mix well, let batter rest about 30 minutes in refrigerator. Turn batter on floured surface and roll $^1/_3$-inch thick. Cut with round cutter and bake 20
minutes at 350°.

Gingersnaps
Corinne Perkins

$^1/_2$ cup shortening
$^1/_4$ cup margarine, soft
1 cup sugar
1 egg
$^1/_4$ cup molasses

2 cups flour
1 tsp ground ginger
2 tsp baking soda
1 tsp cinnamon
$^1/_2$ tsp salt

Cream shortening, margarine and sugar; then add egg and molasses. Mix well. Sift dry ingredients and stir into batter. Shape into small balls and roll in sugar. Place on cookie sheet and bake 10 to 12 minutes at 350°, being careful not to overbake. Gingersnaps are done when soft and puffy.

Grammy Moody's Hermits
Nellie Moody Jones

1 cup sugar
$^1/_2$ cup margarine or shortening
2 eggs
$^1/_2$ cup buttermilk
1 tsp baking soda
1 cup raisins, chopped

3 cups flour
$^1/_2$ tsp cinnamon
1 tsp salt
$^1/_2$ tsp nutmeg
$^1/_2$ tsp cloves

Cream together sugar and shortening. Add eggs and buttermilk and mix thoroughly. Sift dry ingredients and stir into batter, then fold in chopped raisins. Drop by teaspoons onto greased cookie sheet. Bake 12 to 15 minutes at 350°.

Oatmeal Hermits
Freda Genthner

1 cup sugar
1 cup shortening, melted
2 eggs
$^1/_2$ cup milk
2 cups rolled oats

$^3/_4$ tsp baking soda
1 tsp cinnamon
2 scant cups flour
1 cup whole raisins

Combine sugar with melted shortening, stir in eggs and milk, add dry ingredients. Mix, stir in raisins. Leave in refrigerator overnight. Drop by spoonfuls on ungreased cookie sheet. Bake at 400° for 8 to 12 minutes.

Cream-filled Oatmeal Cookies
Debbie Moody Bellows

$1/2$ cup shortening	$1/4$ tsp ginger
$3/4$ cup brown sugar	$1/4$ tsp cloves
2 eggs	1 scant tsp salt
$1/3$ cup molasses	2 cups rolled oats
1 tsp baking soda	$1\,3/4$ cups wheat or white flour
$1/2$ tsp cinnamon	$1/4$ cup milk

Cream together shortening and brown sugar. Beat in eggs and molasses. Add baking soda, spices and salt. Mix well. Stir in oats, flour and milk. Drop batter by the spoonful onto greased cookie sheet. Flatten with fork and bake 10 to 12 minutes at 350°.

Oatmeal Cookie Filling:

$1/3$ cup shortening	1 heaping cup powdered sugar
3 heaping Tbsp Marshmallow Fluff	milk

Combine all ingredients and mix well, adding enough milk to make filling spreadable. Put two cookies together with filling in between.

Chewy Oatmeal Cookies
Nancy Moody Genthner

$3/4$ cup shortening, soft	$1/2$ tsp salt
$1\,1/3$ cups brown sugar	1 tsp cinnamon
2 eggs	$1/4$ tsp nutmeg
1 tsp vanilla	2 cups rolled oats
1 cup flour	1 cup raisins
$3/4$ tsp baking soda	

Cream shortening, sugar, eggs and vanilla. Sift flour, baking soda, salt, cinnamon and nutmeg and add to mixture. Stir in rolled oats and raisins. Drop by spoonfuls on greased cookie sheet. Bake at 350° for 10 to 12 minutes.

Oatmeal Plus Cookies
Debbie Moody Bellows

$^1/_2$ cup sugar
$^1/_2$ cup brown sugar
$^1/_2$ cup shortening
2 eggs
1 tsp vanilla
2 ripe bananas, mashed

$^1/_2$ cup margarine
2 cups rolled oats
1$^1/_2$ cups flour
1 tsp baking soda
1 cup chocolate chips
$^1/_4$ cup peanut butter

Cream together sugars, shortening, eggs, vanilla and bananas. Stir in remaining ingredients and mix well. Drop batter by the spoonful onto cookie sheet and bake 10 to 15 minutes at 375°. Peanut butter chips, butterscotch bits or coconut can be substituted for chocolate chips.

Canadian Oatmeal Shortbread
Judy Moody Beck

1 cup margarine
$^1/_2$ cup packed brown sugar
1 tsp vanilla

1 cup flour
$^1/_2$ tsp baking soda
2 cups rolled oats

Mix margarine, brown sugar and vanilla until fluffy. Blend together flour, baking soda and oats, and stir into mixture. Chill 1 to 2 hours.

Roll $^1/_4$-inch thick, cut with cookie cutter and bake at 350° for 10 to 12 minutes.

Aunt Bertha's "By Cracky" Bars
Eleanor Chase

1 cup sugar
$^3/_4$ cup shortening
2 eggs
1 tsp vanilla
$^1/_3$ cup milk
1$^3/_4$ cups flour
1 tsp salt

$^1/_4$ tsp baking soda
$^1/_2$ cup chopped nuts
1 square unsweetened chocolate, melted
6 to 10 whole graham crackers
1 (6 oz.) pkg. semisweet chocolate chips

Cream together sugar, shortening, eggs and vanilla. Add milk and mix well. Sift dry ingredients and stir into eggs, add milk, and stir. Pour $^1/_3$ of the batter into a small bowl and add melted chocolate and nuts. Spread into a greased 13 x 9 inch baking pan. Layer graham crackers on top. Mix chocolate chips into remaining batter and spread over crackers. Bake 25 minutes at 375°. Cool and cut into squares. (*These bars get a little dry if overcooked.*)

Coffee Squares
Cathy Hopler

2 eggs
2²/₃ cups light brown sugar
1 cup oil
1 cup warm coffee
3 cups flour

1 tsp baking soda
1 tsp salt
1 (12 oz.) pkg. semisweet chocolate chips
1 cup chopped walnuts

Beat eggs in a large bowl, add sugar and oil and mix well. Stir in coffee, flour, soda and salt. Mix thoroughly and pour into a greased 13 x 9 inch pan. Top with chocolate chips and walnuts. Bake 35 to 40 minutes at 350°.

Chocolate Crinkles
Corinne Perkins

¹/₂ cup oil
2 cups sugar
4 squares unsweetened chocolate, melted
4 eggs

2 tsp vanilla
2 cups flour, sifted
2 tsp baking powder
¹/₂ tsp salt
powdered sugar

Mix oil and sugar together, stir in melted chocolate. Beat in eggs, one at a time. Add vanilla and stir in flour, baking powder and salt. Chill batter several hours in refrigerator before using; overnight is best.

Drop by the spoonful into powdered sugar and roll to coat. Place cookies 2 inches apart on greased cookie sheet. Bake 10 to 12 minutes at 350°, being careful not to overbake.

Cocoa Drop Cookies

Brenda Post

$^1/_2$ cup shortening
1 egg
1 cup sugar
$^3/_4$ cup milk
1 tsp vanilla

$^1/_2$ cup cocoa
$^1/_2$ tsp salt
$^1/_2$ tsp baking soda
$1^3/_4$ cups flour, sifted

Beat together shortening, egg and sugar. Stir in milk and vanilla. Sift remaining ingredients, add to batter and mix thoroughly. Chill at least 1 hour.

Drop batter by the spoonful onto greased baking sheet about 2 inches apart, and bake 8 to 10 minutes at 400°.

Carol's Chocolate Squares

Judy Moody Beck

1 cup margarine or butter
4 Tbsp cocoa
1 cup water
2 cups flour

2 cups sugar
2 eggs, beaten
1 tsp vanilla

Combine margarine, cocoa and water in saucepan and bring to a boil; remove from stove and add flour, sugar, beaten eggs and vanilla. Pour into greased 13 x 9 inch pan and bake 20 minutes at 400°. Remove from oven and frost while hot.

Frosting:

1 stick margarine
4 Tbsp cocoa
4 Tbsp milk

1 box powdered sugar
1 tsp vanilla
$^1/_2$ cup nuts

Place margarine, cocoa and milk in saucepan and bring to a boil. Remove from heat and quickly mix in sugar, vanilla and nuts. Spread over hot cake, then cool and cut in squares.

Quick and Easy Brownies
Nancy L. Moody

1/3 cup margarine, softened
1 cup sugar
2 eggs
2 squares unsweetened chocolate, melted

1/2 cup flour
1/4 tsp salt
1 tsp vanilla
1 cup chopped walnuts

In large bowl, cream margarine and sugar. Add eggs, melted chocolate, flour, salt, vanilla and nuts. Pour batter into greased and floured 8-inch-square baking pan. Bake 30 minutes at 300°. (These brownies are best underbaked a little.)

Chunky Brownies with Crust
Marge Adams

1 1/4 cups flour
1/4 cup sugar
1/2 cup cold margarine
1 (14 oz.) can sweetened condensed milk
1/4 cup cocoa

1 egg
1/2 tsp baking powder
1 tsp vanilla
1 (8 oz.) bar milk chocolate candy, broken into chunks
3/4 cup chopped nuts

In medium bowl, combine 1 cup flour and sugar. Cut in margarine until mixture is crumbly. Press crumbs firmly on bottom of 13 x 9 inch pan and bake 15 minutes at 350°.

In larger bowl, beat together milk, cocoa, egg, remaining flour, baking powder and vanilla. Stir in chocolate chunks and nuts and spread batter over prepared and baked crust. Bake 30 minutes or until center is set. Cool and sprinkle with powdered sugar. To store, keep brownies tightly covered at room temperature.

Seven-Layer Bars
Cathy Hopler

1 stick margarine
1 cup graham cracker crumbs
1 cup coconut
1 (12 oz.) pkg. chocolate chips

1 (12 oz.) pkg. butterscotch bits
1 can condensed milk
1/2 cup walnuts

Melt margarine and pour in bottom of 9 x 13 inch baking pan. Sprinkle over margarine: graham cracker crumbs, coconut, chocolate chips, and butterscotch bits. Pour condensed milk over top and sprinkle with nuts. Bake 30 minutes at 350°.

Dump Bars
Debbie Moody Bellows

1 lb. box brown sugar	4 eggs, unbeaten
1 tsp vanilla	2 cups flour
1 stick margarine	1 tsp baking powder
¹/₂ tsp salt	1 (12 oz.) pkg. chocolate chips

Place sugar, vanilla, margarine, salt and eggs in saucepan and heat until margarine is melted. Remove from heat and add flour and baking powder. Stir in chocolate chips. Pour into 9 x 13 inch pan and bake at 350° for 30 minutes. Frost, if desired.

You can also add chopped nuts, dates, raisins or coconut.

Jam & Nut Cookies
Nancy Moody Genthner

1 cup butter	1 tsp salt
1 cup brown sugar	1 cup chopped nuts
2 eggs, separated	strawberry jam
2 cups flour	

Cream butter and brown sugar. Add egg yolks, flour and salt. Roll dough into small balls, flatten and dip in unbeaten egg white and then into chopped nuts. Place on ungreased cookie sheet, bake for 8 minutes at 375°. Take out of oven and press indention in each cookie, fill with strawberry jam and then put back in oven for 10 minutes.

Date Crumbles
Debbie Moody Bellows

²/₃ cup margarine
1¹/₄ cups flour
1¹/₄ cups rolled oats

1 cup brown sugar
1 tsp baking soda

Cut margarine into flour until crumbly. Add remaining ingredients and mix well. Press ¹/₂ of crumb mixture into greased 9-inch square pan. Spread with date filling. Cover with remaining crumb mixture. Bake at 350° for 30 minutes.

Date Filling:

¹/₂ cup chopped dates
¹/₂ cup cold water

2 Tbsp brown sugar

Combine all ingredients, cook about 5 to 7 minutes. Add more water if needed. Cool.

These may be filled with your favorite mincemeat instead of dates.

Mom's Old-fashioned Filled Cookies
Nancy Moody Genthner

1 cup sugar
¹/₂ cup shortening
1 egg
¹/₂ cup milk

1 tsp vanilla
3 cups flour
1 tsp salt
2¹/₂ tsp baking powder

Combine and cream sugar and shortening. Beat in egg, milk and vanilla. Sift dry ingredients, add to batter and mix well. Roll dough to ¹/₄ inch thick and cut cookies with round cutter. Put cookies on large cookie sheet and drop filling into the center of each. Top with second cookie and seal edges lightly. Bake 10 minutes at 350°.

Date Filling:

1 (8 oz.) box chopped dates
¹/₂ cup water
¹/₃ cup sugar

1 Tbsp flour
¹/₂ tsp salt
¹/₂ tsp vanilla

Combine all ingredients and cook over medium heat until thickened.

Date Balls
Nancy Moody Genthner

1 cup chopped dates
1 cup sugar
$^1/_4$ cup shortening

1 egg, beaten
$2^1/_2$ cups Rice Krispies
grated coconut or powdered sugar

Combine and boil sugar, dates, shortening and egg until sugar completely dissolves—about two minutes. Remove from heat and stir in Rice Krispies. Mix well. When mixture cools enough to handle, shape into walnut-sized balls. Roll in coconut or powdered sugar.

Whoopie Pies
Susan Moody

$^3/_4$ cup margarine
$1^1/_2$ cups sugar
2 eggs
$^1/_2$ tsp vanilla
$1^1/_2$ cups milk

3 cups flour
$^3/_4$ cup cocoa
$^3/_4$ tsp baking powder
$2^1/_4$ tsp baking soda
$^1/_2$ tsp salt

In large bowl, cream margarine, sugar, eggs and vanilla. Add milk slowly and mix well. Combine dry ingredients and stir into batter. Drop batter by the teaspoon onto a greased cookie sheet and bake 15 minutes at 350°. Cool, then fill with any of the Whoopie Pie fillings on pps 158–59.

Cathy's Whoopie Pies
Cathy Hopler

2 eggs, separated
$^1/_2$ cup shortening
1 cup sugar
5 Tbsp cocoa
2 cups flour

1 tsp baking powder
1 tsp baking soda
1 tsp salt
1 cup milk
1 tsp vanilla

Beat egg yolks until lightly colored. Cream together shortening and s ugar, add egg yolks. Sift dry ingredients and add to creamed mixture with milk and vanilla. Drop by teaspoonfuls onto ungreased cookie sheets. Bake at 375° for 8 to 10 minutes, depending on the size of the cookie. Put together with the following filling.

Cream Filling:

2 egg whites
2 cups confectioner's sugar
1/2 cup shortening

1/4 tsp salt
1 tsp vanilla

Beat egg whites until stiff, add 1/4 cup confectioner's sugar and beat. Cream shortening and rest of confectioner's sugar, add salt and vanilla. Stir in egg white mixture and mix until smooth, about 2 minutes.

Molasses Whoopie Pies
Nellie Moody Jones

1 cup shortening
1 cup sugar
1 tsp salt
2 eggs
1 cup molasses
1 tsp vinegar

4 1/2 cups flour
1 tsp cinnamon
1 tsp ground ginger
2 tsp baking soda
1 cup hot, strong coffee

Combine and cream shortening, sugar and salt. Add eggs, molasses and vinegar and mix thoroughly. In separate bowl, sift together flour, cinnamon and ginger and stir into batter. Dissolve baking soda in hot coffee and add to remaining ingredients. Drop by teaspoonful onto a greased cooked sheet and bake 15 minutes at 350°. Cool and fill with whoopie pie filling.

Whoopie Pie Filling:

1/2 cup shortening
6 Tbsp Marshmallow Fluff

2 cups powdered sugar
milk

Combine all ingredients and beat thoroughly, add just enough milk to make filling spreadable.

Grammy Hill's Pumpkin Whoopie Pies
Cathy Hopler

1 (16 oz.) can pumpkin
2 cups sugar
1 cup oil
2 eggs, beaten
4 cups flour
4 tsp baking powder

2 tsp cinnamon
1 tsp salt
1 tsp nutmeg
2 tsp baking soda
2 tsp milk

Mix all ingredients together, either by hand or electric mixer until well moistened. Place by spoonful on ungreased cookie sheets. You should get 48 single pies. Bake at 375° for 10 to 13 minutes. Remove from cookie sheets and cool on wire racks.

Filling:

2²/₃ cups confectioner's sugar
1 cup Marshmallow Fluff
1¹/₂ tsp vanilla

1 cup shortening
¹/₃ cup milk

Combine all ingredients until smooth. Spread filling generously between two pies and sandwich together.

Cynthia's Peanut Butter Cookies
Nancy Moody Genthner

¹/₂ cup sugar
¹/₂ cup brown sugar
¹/₂ cup margarine
1 egg
¹/₂ cup peanut butter

1¹/₂ cups flour
1 tsp baking soda
¹/₄ tsp salt
¹/₄ tsp powder

Cream together sugars and margarine, then beat in egg and peanut butter. Mix in dry ingredients. Drop batter by teaspoonful onto ungreased cooked sheet and flatten slightly with fork. Bake 8 to 10 minutes at 350°.

Double Peanut Butter Cookies
Judy Moody Beck

2 cups flour
1 cup sugar
1 tsp baking soda
¹/₂ tsp salt
1 cup quick oatmeal

1 cup margarine or butter
1 cup creamy peanut butter
2 Tbsp milk
¹/₂ cup light corn syrup
crunchy peanut butter

Sift together dry ingredients, stir in oatmeal. Using pastry blender, cut in margarine and creamy peanut butter until ingredients resemble cornmeal. Blend in corn syrup and milk. Shape dough into 2 rolls and chill. (I shape mine so the cookies will be rectangular when cut.) Slice chilled dough ¹/₄ inch thick and place half the slices on ungreased cookie sheet. Spread dough slices with ¹/₂ tsp crunchy peanut butter and cover with second slice. Bake 8 to 10 minutes at 350°, being careful not to overbake. Cool slightly before removing cookies from pan.

Peanut Butter Bars
Nancy Moody Genthner

$^1/_2$ cup shortening
$^1/_2$ cup sugar
$^1/_2$ cup brown sugar
$^1/_3$ cup peanut butter
1 tsp vanilla
1 egg, beaten

$^1/_4$ cup milk
1 cup flour
$^1/_2$ tsp baking soda
$^1/_2$ tsp salt
1 cup rolled oats

In large bowl, cream shortening, sugars, peanut butter and vanilla. Add beaten egg and milk, and mix well. Sift together dry ingredients and stir into batter. Pour into 8-inch-square pan and bake 20 to 25 minutes at 350°. Cool and frost with Cocoa Frosting.

Cocoa Frosting:

2 cups powdered sugar
$^1/_4$ cup cocoa
3 Tbsp margarine

2 to 3 Tbsp boiling water
$^1/_2$ tsp vanilla

Combine all ingredients and beat until creamy.

Salted Peanut Cookies
Jean Moody

2 eggs
2 cups packed brown sugar
$1^1/_2$ cups margarine, melted
$1^1/_2$ cups salted Spanish peanuts
$2^1/_2$ cups flour

1 tsp baking soda
1 tsp baking powder
$^1/_2$ tsp salt
3 cups rolled oats
1 cup cornflakes

Combine eggs and sugar, beat well. Blend in melted margarine, then stir in peanuts. Set aside. Sift flour, soda, baking powder and salt into large bowl. Add rolled oats and cornflakes. Stir dry ingredients into batter and mix well. Drop by the spoonful onto greased cookie sheets and bake 8 to 10 minutes at 400°. Remove cookies from pan at once.

Peanut Butter Fingers
Norma Moody Dion

$^1/_2$ cup margarine
$^1/_2$ cup brown sugar
$^1/_2$ cup sugar
1 egg
$^1/_3$ cup peanut butter
$^1/_2$ tsp baking soda

$^1/_4$ tsp salt
1 cup flour
$^1/_2$ tsp vanilla
1 cup quick-cooking rolled oats
1 (6 oz.) pkg. semisweet chocolate
    chips

Cream margarine and sugars, blend in egg and peanut butter. Add dry ingredients and oats and mix well. Spread dough in ungreased 9 x 13 inch pan. Bake 20 to 25 minutes at 350°. Do not overbake.

Remove from oven and sprinkle with chocolate chips. Let stand 5 minutes, allowing the chips to melt and spread.

Cocoa Frosting:

Combine $^1/_2$ cup powdered sugar, 2 Tbsp peanut butter and 2 Tbsp milk and spread over top after chocolate has firmed up. Cut in squares.

Chocolate Chip Cookies
Nancy Moody Genthner

$^2/_3$ cup shortening/softened butter
$^1/_2$ cup sugar
$^1/_2$ cup packed brown sugar
1 egg
1 tsp vanilla

$1^1/_2$ cups flour
$^1/_2$ tsp baking soda
$^1/_2$ tsp salt
$^1/_2$ cup chopped nuts, optional
1 (6 oz.) pkg. semisweet chocolate
    chips

Cream sugars and shortening/butter combination. Add egg and vanilla. Stir in dry ingredients. Add chocolate chips and nuts. Drop rounded teaspoonfuls on ungreased baking sheet. Bake at 350° for 10 to 12 minutes. Cookies should still be soft when removed from oven.

100 Good Cookies
Charlene Moody Ward

1 egg	1 tsp vanilla
1 cup oil	3^1/$_2$ cups flour
1 cup margarine	1 tsp baking soda
1 cup brown sugar	1 tsp cream of tartar
1 cup granulated sugar	1 cup Rice Krispies
1 cup chocolate chips	1 cup rolled oats
1 cup chopped walnuts	

Cream together egg, oil, margarine and sugars. Add remaining ingredients and mix well. Drop batter by the spoonful onto ungreased baking sheets and bake 12 to 15 minutes at 350°.

Coconut, butterscotch bits, peanut butter bits or raisins can be substituted for the chocolate chips, walnuts, or both.

This recipe may be made substituting 1 cup of honey for the sugars, increasing the flour to 4 cups and the oatmeal to 2 cups.

Raspberry Chews
Margaret Moody Wellman

^{3}/$_4$ cup margarine	1 cup chopped walnuts
^{3}/$_4$ cup sugar	1 cup raspberry preserves
2 eggs, separated	^{1}/$_2$ cup flaked coconut
1^1/$_2$ cups flour	

In large bowl, combine margarine with ^{1}/$_4$ cup sugar and beat until fluffy. Beat in egg yolks, blend in flour and spread in a 13 x 9 baking pan. Bake 15 minutes at 350° or until crust is golden brown. Remove from oven and set aside. In separate bowl, beat egg whites until foamy and doubled in volume. Beat in remaining sugar until meringue stands in firm peaks and fold in walnuts. Set aside. Spread raspberry preserves over baked crust and sprinkle with coconut. Spread meringue over raspberry-coconut layer and bake 25 minutes at 350°. Cool and cut into squares.

Sugar Cookies
Cathy Hopler

2 cups flour
1$^{1}/_{2}$ tsp baking powder
$^{1}/_{2}$ tsp salt
$^{1}/_{2}$ cup butter or margarine

$^{3}/_{4}$ cup sugar
1 egg
1 tsp vanilla
1 Tbsp milk

Mix together flour, baking powder and salt. In separate bowl, cream together butter and sugar; add egg and beat until smooth and fluffy. Stir in vanilla and milk. Add flour mixture and blend thoroughly. Chill cookie dough until easy to handle. Roll out to $^{1}/_{4}$-inch thickness on lightly floured board. Cut with cookie cutter and bake at 375° for 6 to 10 minutes.

Ethel's Sugar Cookies
Nancy Moody Genthner

$^{3}/_{4}$ cup shortening or butter, softened
1 cup sugar
2 eggs
$^{1}/_{2}$ tsp vanilla or lemon flavoring

2$^{1}/_{2}$ cups flour
1 tsp baking powder
1 tsp salt

Cream shortening or butter combination and sugar, add eggs and flavoring. Stir in sifted dry ingredients. Chill dough at least 1 hour.

Roll out $^{1}/_{8}$-inch thick. Cut in desired shapes and place on ungreased cookie sheet. Sprinkle with colored sugar if desired. Bake 6 to 8 minutes at 375°.

Stir-N-Drop Sugar Cookies
Nancy Moody Genthner

2 eggs
$^{2}/_{3}$ cup oil
1 tsp vanilla or lemon flavoring
$^{3}/_{4}$ cup sugar

2 cups flour
2 tsp baking powder
$^{1}/_{2}$ tsp salt

Beat eggs and stir in oil and vanilla. Blend in sugar until mixture thickens. Sift dry ingredients and stir in. Drop by teaspoonfuls on ungreased baking sheet. Flatten with greased bottom of glass dipped in sugar. Bake 8 to 10 minutes at 375°.

Pineapple Sponge Cookies
Deborah Pooley

$^1/_3$ cup shortening
$^2/_3$ cup sugar
1 egg
1$^1/_3$ cups flour

$^1/_2$ tsp baking soda
$^1/_4$ tsp salt
$^1/_2$ cup crushed pineapple
1 tsp lemon extract

Cream shortening with sugar and beat in egg. Sift flour with baking soda and salt and add to creamed batter. Fold in pineapple and lemon flavoring and mix lightly. Drop by the teaspoonful onto a greased cookie sheet and bake 12 minutes at 400°.

Coconut Pineapple Squares
Hannah Flagg

1$^1/_4$ cups crushed pineapple, drained
1 cup coconut
$^1/_2$ cup shortening
$^3/_4$ cup sugar
2 eggs
$^1/_4$ tsp ginger

2 cups flour
$^1/_4$ tsp salt
$^1/_2$ tsp baking soda
2 to 3 Tbsp pineapple juice
1 (6 oz.) pkg. semisweet chocolate
    chips

Mix together $^1/_2$ cup pineapple and coconut to make topping and set aside. Cream shortening, sugar and eggs. Sift dry ingredients and add to creamed ingredients. Stir in remaining pineapple and pineapple juice. Add chocolate chips. Spread batter in greased and floured 9 x 13 inch pan and spread with topping. Bake 30 minutes at 350°. Cool and cut in squares.

Candy & Snacks

Peanut Butter Balls
Sheri Beck

1 cup margarine
¹/₂ cup peanut butter
¹/₂ cup chopped nuts
1 tsp vanilla

1 (1 lb.) box powdered sugar
1 (12 oz.) pkg. semisweet chocolate
  chips
²/₃ cup grated paraffin

Melt margarine in medium saucepan. Add remaining ingredients, except chocolate and paraffin. Shape candy into small balls and chill. Melt together chocolate and paraffin in double boiler over hot—not boiling—water. Using two forks, dip peanut butter balls in chocolate and set on wax paper to dry.

Brown Sugar Peanut Butter Fudge
Harriet Hilton

³/₄ cup milk
2 cups sugar
2¹/₂ cups brown sugar

1 small jar peanut butter
1 (7 oz.) jar Marshmallow Fluff

Boil together milk and sugars for 5 minutes. Remove from heat and add peanut butter and marshmallow. Spread in 9 x 13 inch pan and refrigerate until cool.

Peanut Butter Fudge
Sheri Beck

¹/₃ cup milk
1¹/₂ cups sugar
6 Tbsp margarine

¹/₂ cup peanut butter
¹/₂ cup Marshmallow Fluff
¹/₄ cup chopped nuts, optional

Boil together milk, margarine and sugar for 4 minutes. Add peanut butter, marshmallow and chopped nuts. Stir to mix and spread in 8-inch-square pan. Chill until firm.

Three-Minute Fudge
Brenda Post

1 cup sugar
2 Tbsp cornstarch
1 Tbsp cocoa

$^1/_2$ cup milk
3 Tbsp margarine
1 tsp vanilla

Combine sugar, cornstarch, cocoa, milk and margarine, and boil 3 minutes. Remove from heat, add vanilla and beat well. Pour into greased 8-inch-square pan and chill until firm.

Reese's Squares
Judy Moody Beck

1 (18 oz.) jar peanut butter
1 (9 oz.) jar honey
non-fat dried milk
1 cup sugar

5 Tbsp margarine or butter
$^1/_3$ cup milk
1 (6 oz.) pkg. semisweet chocolate
  chips

Blend together peanut butter and honey. Mix in dried milk until stiff. Press into 9 x 13 inch pan. In saucepan, combine sugar, margarine and milk. Bring to a boil, stirring constantly for 1 minute. Remove from heat, stir in chocolate chips and blend until smooth. Spread over peanut butter and honey and refrigerate until firm. Cut in squares.

Crunch Candy
Rebecca Little

1 cup butter
1 cup sugar
2 Tbsp water

$^1/_4$ tsp salt
1 large milk chocolate bar
1 cup chopped nuts

Combine butter, sugar, water and salt in saucepan and heat, stirring constantly, to 300° on candy thermometer—or until mixture forms a brittle ball when dropped in cold water. Remove from heat and pour onto large, greased cookie sheet that has been warmed in the oven. Sprinkle chopped nuts and chocolate pieces on top. Cool and break into pieces.

Mom's Party Mix
Judy Moody Beck

1/2 cup margarine
4 tsp Worcestershire sauce
1 tsp seasoned salt
2 cups Rice Chex
2 cups Corn Chex
2 cups Wheat Chex

2 cups Kix cereal
2 cups Cheerios
2 cups Chinese noodles
2 cups thin pretzels
1 cup salted peanuts

Over low heat, melt together margarine, Worcestershire sauce and seasoned salt. Mix cereals and peanuts in large bowl and pour melted margarine over them. Stir well and pour mix onto greased cookie sheet. Bake 1 hour at 250°, stirring every 15 minutes.

Easy Granola
Christine Reed

6 cups old-fashioned oats
1 cup sunflower seeds, raw
1 cup chopped or slivered almonds
1 tsp cinnamon

1/2 cup oil
2/3 cup honey
1 cup raisins, optional

Combine all ingredients except raisins and spread on greased cookie sheet. Bake at 300° for 30 minutes, stirring every 10 minutes. After baking, immediately scrape into bowl to cool. Add raisins.

You can use any combination of oats (at least 4 cups), seeds, nuts or coconut.

Complimentary—and practical—
Moody's Diner calendars from
1930 (below) and 1940 (left).

MOODY'S DINER THROUGH THE YEARS

Part II

Growing Up Moody: Warren's Stories
Moody People • Moody Travelers
A Moody Wedding

Waldoboro's version of Our Gang, 1935
Left to right: Dewey, Alvah and Warren Moody, cousin Bevy Eaton,
David and Nellie Moody (Jones).

Growing Up Moody
Warren's Stories

HOT PANTS

I was a curious little guy, the kind that has to take an alarm clock apart to see how it works and then can't get it to work again once put back together. I was always getting involved in Dad's various construction projects, and frequently not by invitation!

When I was five or six years old, I was closely observing the construction of some new overnight cabins up on the hill. Several foundation holes had been dug, about two feet in diameter and four feet deep, for prefab concrete posts. Rain had partially filled the postholes, and Oscar Smith and his brother Boop were bailing out the muddy water. Oscar liked me, and I thought of him as my buddy, but Boop barely tolerated me. Our relationship was more like Dennis the Menace and Mr. Wilson.

I was giving Boop a hard time, intentionally getting in his way. Boop responded by whacking the back of my bare legs with a long, slender stick. When Boop bent over to scoop up another bucket of muddy water, I decided to return the favor. His rear end was an excellent target, and the stick made contact on the right hip pocket.

Boop was a pipe smoker and carried a generous supply of big wooden kitchen matches in his pocket. You guessed it, the very same pocket that just got smacked.

Warren, "a curious little guy," resisting the hammocks and bunkhouse behind him.

Dewey Moody: WWII
Navy veteran and
nocturnal wanderer.

Combustion occurred, followed by a wild dance that was punctuated with words a little boy's ears should not hear. The dancer ended the show with a splendid leap into a muddy puddle and sat in the cooling ooze.

This display attracted considerable attention. Dad rushed over. "What the thunder is going on, Oscar?" Oscar stopped laughing long enough to reply, "Percy, in all my fifty years, I've never seen Boop move so fast."

A THUMP IN THE NIGHT

Our oldest brother, Dewey, was in the Navy during WWII and served on a destroyer-repair base in New Guinea. While there, he suffered what the Navy described as a severe case of heat stroke and was discharged. He returned home and moved into the bunkhouse with the rest of us boys prior to resuming his studies at the University of Maine.

Dad had built the bunkhouse a few years prior. Its purpose was to get the boys out of the main house and give Mom some relief during the busy summer season. There were six bunks, stacked three per side. The middle bunk was about five feet above the floor, and the top one at close to nose-bleed elevation. All agreed that Dewey should take one of the bottom bunks in case there might be something to this "severe heat-stroke" thing.

It was a beautiful, moonlit summer night when I awoke to a strange repetitive noise. I looked down from my middle bunk to the source of the noise from the opposite bottom bunk. Dewey was leaning over the edge throwing a large hunting knife at some imaginary beast on the floor and mumbling a lot of four-letter words. I was about to yell at Dewey, but figured if I startled him, that big old knife might come flying my way. As my eyes became more accustomed to the moonlit room, I realized that Dewey's eyes were closed. He was still asleep!

Everyone else in the bunkhouse was sound asleep. I was trying to figure out what to do when Dewey—still asleep—got up, strapped on an old cartridge belt and started out the door. The warrior off to battle. The uniform of the day—boxer undershorts! I eased out of my bunk, quickly dressed and cautiously followed.

Dewey walked down the path through the field behind the bunkhouse and then out onto the highway.

He then proceeded down the middle of the road toward the railroad crossing at the foot of the hill. I followed at a safe distance. As we got close to the tracks, a car coming from the other direction flashed its lights and blew its horn. Dewey dutifully stepped to the side of the road and onto the shoulder. The road gravel under his bare feet did what I dared not do, and suddenly Dewey was awake.

On the way back, we decided to hide all knives, guns and any other potential weapons. We locked the bunkhouse door and hid the key, and then alerted our bunkmates to Dewey's apparent penchant for nocturnal strolls. The precautions helped, but there were still occasional short trips.

Passage of time and life in old, familiar surroundings seemed to eventually solve the problem. Dewey returned to college that fall, and as far as we know, there were no reported nocturnal sightings of a strange warrior in or around Orono.

THE GROCERY WAGON

Dad had just purchased a large parcel of land running east from the pond by the diner, up the hill across the railroad tracks, and along the large field and some distance over the ledges into the woods. It had a big, old weather-beaten barn that stood at the crest of the hill a bit west of the railroad tracks. We had conjured up all sorts of scary things about that old barn, and when Dad invited us to go inspect the place with him, we were excited but apprehensive.

The two great doors swung open revealing a dusty cavern with millions of cobwebs and a scattering of old, musty hay. As our eyes adjusted to the semidarkness, we saw that several pieces of farm equipment had been stored under the parallel haylofts on either side of the barn floor.

This wasn't the exact grocery wagon we demolished, but a similar one.

The one that caught the eyes of us young boys was a pristine grocery wagon. Dad was quick to pick up on our interest and told us in no uncertain terms it was off-limits—absolutely off-limits; do not touch; don't even think of it!

For readers of the newer generation, a description of a grocery wagon might be helpful. In the terms of the day, a grocery wagon might best be described as a one-horse, power-roadster pickup. It was a lightweight, large-wheel, one-horse wagon with a full-width seat at the front and a platform body at the rear. It was also equipped with rear-wheel brakes to make life easier for the horse on long downhill grades. To apply the brakes, the driver pulled a lever that rotated two arms to the rim of the rear wheels. The friction surface was a hard wood block attached to the end of the brake arms.

Boys being boys, it wasn't long before we saw an opportunity to take the wagon out for a spin. Dad had gone to Rockland to pick up supplies for the diner, and we knew he would be gone for at least two hours. So Alvah, David and I gathered the gang: Chappy (Warren Chapman) and the Achorns (Austin, Elmer and Geraldine). We seven young explorers were off for a ride in the forbidden grocery wagon—down from the barn, around the pond and up to the top of the hill by the cabins. Once up on the hill, we were careful not to come around the barn since that would put us in view of the kitchen windows, and Mom might see us.

After a few spins, we figured it best to get the wagon back to where it belonged and so headed back down the hill. To speed our return, we had Chappy steering up front, holding the shafts where the horse belonged. Alvah sat in the seat manning the brakes, with Geraldine by his side. Elmer and Austin stood on the platform body, holding on to the back of the front seat, and David and I pushed at the rear. As the wagon started down the hill toward the diner it rapidly picked up speed, and both pushers jumped to the back of the wagon and sat facing the rear with legs hanging over the back.

In a matter of seconds we were going downhill like the proverbial bat. Chappy's feet were trying to keep up with the speed of the wagon, but were rapidly losing out to the forces of gravity.

Chappy yelled, "PUT ON THE BRAKES!" Alvah yanked the lever, but we were still accelerating. I looked at the brake block that was supposed to be rubbing on the wheel rim, anticipating a cloud of smoke created by the friction. No smoke, no friction, no brake block contacting the wheel rim. The wheel was there, so were the blocks, but they were warped and not touching.

"The brakes don't work!" Alvah yelled to Chappy. Chappy, realizing he was soon to be run over by the wagon, shouted back that he was going to turn down the spring road.

The spring road was a two-rut dirt track that turned off at a right angle to the road we were currently traversing at such speed, heading downhill toward the diner. Not only was the spring road not much of a road, it was bounded on both sides by wild raspberry bushes, a stone wall and lots of trees. We all thought Chappy's decision was a stroke of genius, that the spring road was our salvation. This was a not to be so.

Chappy made the turn, but his feet didn't make it over the hump between the ruts. As he fell he pulled the shafts down with him, and they buried themselves in the ground like two spears hurled by an ancient warrior. The wagon flipped over, sending its occupants flying in a great cloud of dust, sod and tangled raspberry bushes.

I recall coming to and looking up at a wagon wheel rotating in the sky with the sun reflecting off the spokes just like we had seen in the Westerns at the Waldo Theatre. I heard lots of moaning and some mumblings I couldn't understand. Elmer was hanging upside down, his foot caught in the crotch of a tree. He had lost his false teeth in the crash, hence the mumbles. We found his teeth still intact and checked each other for broken bones. Other than lots of scratches and bruises, all but the wagon had survived. Yes, the wagon did not fare so well, but that is another story.

TARZAN

The Saturday afternoon double features at the Waldo Theatre were usually two Westerns, or a Western and a Tarzan movie—both very exciting for a bunch of young boys with visions of great adventures. We couldn't do much to emulate the cowboy shoot-em-ups, but swinging from vines (ropes in our case) was a real possibility.

We quickly discovered you can only travel so far swinging from a vine, but sliding down an inclined wire strung between two distant points, now that is a whole new program! There were any number of possible locations on the farm for this activity, hidden from the view of critical senior eyes.

Dad had plenty of wire from an old telegraph line the railroad had removed and left along the right-of-way for the abutting property owners. Dad used it for electric fence and other farm-related jobs requiring a piece of sturdy wire. The top of the icehouse and the peak of the hen house, some thirty feet away, were selected as the best available points for the wire attachment. The top of the icehouse was about ten feet higher than the henhouse. We made a cross stick with a notch cut at the center to ride on the wire and then strung the wire from the icehouse to the henhouse. We fastened the wire with a sag so the feet of the rider would contact the ground before the rest of his body contacted the side of the henhouse.

We oiled the wire and the cross stick to improve the speed of descent. The time had come to pick the first daredevil. Much discussion followed: should the smallest go first, to be sure the wire would hold, or maybe the tallest would be best, to be sure his feet would contact the ground before he hit the henhouse. The tallest won, and Carroll, who was more than six feet tall, was soon perched on the edge of the icehouse. Holding the notched stick in his right hand, he placed it over the wire and then grabbed the other end with his left.

He gave a Tarzan yell and kicked off from the icehouse. Sir Isaac Newton took over, and Carroll accelerated down the wire much faster than any of us had anticipated, Carroll included. As he approached the henhouse, another miscalculation became evident. Even at a good six feet, with both arms extended, he was not going to get his feet ion the ground in time. Carroll realized this and let go of the stick, but not in time. He was in midair, with his arms flailing and his feet clawing for the ground, when he hit the henhouse with a wicked loud thud and then slowly sank to the ground.

We scrambled off the icehouse and ran to Carroll, who was slowly getting to his feet. He looked at all of our startled faces and said, "That's enough Tarzan for me!"

RED BALL SNEAKERS

The roof on the barn by the house was in need of new shingles and Dad hired Sidney Creamer to do the job. I was about fourteen at the time and was dispatched to do the grunt work for Sidney. That was okay. Sidney was a great old guy and working on the roof was better than mowing the lawns and clipping around the cabins with hand shears. The guy that invented those things should have been shot at sundown!

The old wooden shingles had to be stripped off the roof, carried over to the side and dropped to the ground. The roof had a fairly steep pitch but a teenage boy with new Red Ball sneakers could negotiate the roof with no problem. I was stripping the old shingles and Sidney applying the new, working from a single scaffold. We started at the eaves on the west side and worked to the peak, then repeating the process on the east side.

As we approached the peak from the west side, I calculated it would be easier to throw the old shingles just over the peak to the east side rather than constantly having to stop and carry them to the side for disposal. Once all the old shingles were stripped from the west side, I could then clear the pile off the east side. This meant walking around on a bunch of old loose shingles on the east side of the roof, but the new sneakers would take care of that.

"Don't walk around on those loose shingles," Sidney said. But any teenage boy knows a lot more than an old man, and it was obvious Sidney didn't know squat about Red Ball sneakers.

I think the Red Ball sneakers failed on the second step, or maybe it was the third. In any case, I was suddenly on my back, riding down the roof feet-first on a heap of old shingles, heading for the eaves at speed.

At this point, I should mention that the east side of the barn was where the cattle were kept. Hence, it was the location of the manure pile—and a pretty big one at that. Because of its location under the eaves of the barn roof it was always saturated with rain water. Those brand-new Red Ball sneakers made a sickening squishy sound as they penetrated the soupy mess. I was up to my chest when I finally came to a stop, stuck in the manure pile, being showered by old shingles and yelling for help!

Uncle Richard and Dad were in the barn and quickly responded to the ruckus. Hidden under Uncle Richard's calm exterior was a somewhat bizarre sense of humor. He turned to Dad, "Gorry! Do you suppose he is worth saving?"

Dad picked up on it. "It's going to take a lot of clean-up work, but maybe we could salvage those new Red Ball sneakers for one of the other boys," he replied.

Their banter was interrupted by me. "Get me out of here, and quick—I'm still sinking!"

They pushed an old wooden ladder across the pile and I managed to work my way out of the mire and along the ladder to solid footing. Uncle Richard and Dad broke out the garden hose and hosed away the manure. Those Red Ball sneakers were never the same after that.

NEW BARN DOORS

Dad had Sidney Creamer make some new doors for the large barn by our house where the cattle were kept. These were beautiful, large doors of vertical, matched pine that rolled open, exposing the barn floor where hay was unloaded to the haylofts.

Our friend Carroll had just purchased a well-used 1935 Ford V8 sedan. "Henry's marvel" would get up and go quite well, but the stopping part needed help. The four-wheel mechanical brake system needed adjustment.

We motored down to the garage by the diner, jacked up the old Ford and had at it. Early on, we removed the pin connecting the brake pedal to the system, thinking this would allow us to adjust the brakes for equal pres-

Debbie Moody (Bellows) takes time out from playing kick-the-can
to pose in front of the infamous barn doors, 1952.

sure on all four wheels. Once the adjustments are made, the pin is reinstalled and locked in place with a cotter key.

It was time for a test run. Alvah was the test pilot. He buzzed down Route 220 toward town and then turned up the hill on old Route 1, headed home. He pulled in the driveway at speed and headed straight for the barn. As the old Ford approached the barn, Alvah applied the brakes. There was a thud when the pedal hit the floorboard, followed by a second, louder thud when the Ford hit the barn doors, then a sickening crack as the doors buckled inward before finally stopping the car. As we gently rolled the Ford back into the barnyard, Dad's brand new barn doors returned to their original shape—somewhat.

Alvah ran into the house and asked Mom where Dad was. She told him he was taking a nap before heading north to hunt up Christmas trees.

"Should I wake him?" Mom asked.

"No, let him sleep," Alvah answered.

He ran off to find Uncle Richard to help us repair the barn doors. Once the doors were pulled back together and the broken frame spliced on the back side, we turned our attention to the Ford. Seems someone had forgotten the cotter key, and the linkage pin fell out during the trip up from the diner.

The next summer, when we were putting up hay, Dad noticed the splices on the frame of the barn doors and asked me if I knew what had happened to his new doors.

"Well, last spring when Prince [our old work horse] was being shod, he must have got kind of wild and backed into them," I said.

Dad just shook his head. "Blasted horse."

HAYING (AS A TOURIST ATTRACTION)

Our farm had a certain fascination for a lot of the folks from away who stayed at the cabins on the hill. Many children of the cabin guests wanted to see all the animals and get involved in the various farm activities. For some reason, haying was of particular interest and Dad was constantly bugged to let some of the kids go along to the hay fields. The parents of a teenage girl and her younger brother finally broke down Dad's concern about the potential liability, and he agreed to let them go haying with us, one in the back of the truck on the load tramping down the hay with me, and the other inside the truck with farmhand Bill Davis.

Uncle Richard, David Moody and a farm truck. The ice house mentioned in Warren's "Tarzan" story is in the back left of the photo.

The boy decided that riding in the truck with Bill was the cool thing to do, and his sister could help tramp hay. I liked this arrangement. The boy was a little annoying, but his sister was a pretty blonde about my age. Her white shorts and blue v-neck blouse weren't exactly haying attire, but she sure looked nice. I told her that, when the truck was moving in the hay field, she should stand behind and hold on to me as I leaned forward on the pitchfork for balance.

The truck moved between the windrows of hay, stopping periodically while brother David pitched hay up on one side and Uncle Richard on the other. The truck was just about fully loaded and advancing to the next pile of hay. I was leaning on the pitchfork and she was hanging onto me as instructed.

I knew to keep a close eye on the guys on the ground since it was not uncommon for things other than hay to come flying up with the load—and not always by mistake. This day was no exception. Uncle Richard, forgetting for the moment that there was someone else on the load, picked up a foot-long garter snake with his pitchfork and flung it up at me.

I saw it coming and ducked. The snake passed over my head and wrapped itself around the young lady's neck. What a scream she let out! The snake, convinced this was not a good place to hang out, headed for cover in the V of her pretty blue blouse. As his tail disappeared, she tore her blouse off. The snake was probably long gone, but she continued screaming and clothes kept flying.

"What the devil do I do now?" I wondered, realizing I had better do something quick before she fell off the truck and I'd have to explain things to Dad. I held her down in the hay and convinced her the snake was gone.

Hysteria quickly gave way to embarrassment. Clothes were retrieved and life on the hay load returned to some semblance of normalcy. It all happened quickly enough that those on the ground couldn't make out any of the details of what they were hearing. We decided to keep the incident to ourselves—I wouldn't have to explain this to Dad, and she felt that the less her brother knew, the better.

As we rode back to the barn, lying atop the load of hay, both holding the pitchfork for support and each lost in our own thoughts. I was thinking that haying would never be the same, or as exciting. I can barely imagine what she was thinking, but it probably had nothing to do with going haying again.

Right: The Moody boys in 1941(left to right): David, Dewey, Alvah (holding Ginger), Harvey, Warren (not dressed up). Not hard to tell who the troublemaker was.

UNCLE RICHARD FLAGG
by Warren and Harvey

It is impossible to talk about life at our house without mentioning Uncle Richard. He was a cousin on our Dad's side and became our uncle by marriage to Mom's youngest sister. He worked for Dad, managing the farm, milking cows, feeding pigs and chickens, putting up hay, and all the other necessary jobs required on a farm.

Children in the family, and those visiting in the cabins, gravitated to him like he was the pied piper. Part of this was the attraction of the farm, but mostly it was because of who he was. Uncle Richard was the most even-tempered, quiet and gentle person you could ever meet. He had a fine mind and knowledge that extended from the fields of the farm to geography and history. When you were with him, you were treated as an equal, listened to with undivided attention and invited along as he went about his work. (That seems remarkable when we think of how many times we were just plain underfoot and undoubtedly more hindrance than help.)

Best of all, he was our confidant in our many adventures, and when things went astray that might invite the displeasure of Dad, he was the one who helped repair the damage. He lived next door, so was readily available, and would quietly help us out of our mishaps with an amused smile.

There is a line from a poem that always reminds us of Uncle Richard. It goes, "If you can keep your head when all about you people are losing theirs"—that fit him to a T.

No matter what was going on, we knew that if Uncle Richard was there, somehow everything would be okay. This was true with farm critters and wild animals as well as us kids. We offer the following as an example:

One winter we were blessed with a lot of snow, then the January thaw gave us rain, followed by zero-degree weather, resulting in a thick crust over the deep snow bed. We were helping Uncle Richard in the barn when we heard dogs in hot pursuit down in the pasture. "Probably running deer," Uncle Richard said as he picked up his old single-shot 12-gauge and stepped out into the barnyard. A big doe crossed the road and started up the embankment on the other side, heading for the open field. She broke through the crust in the field, and the dogs were circling for the kill. A blast of buckshot in the air sent the dogs on their way, leaving behind the exhausted doe, bleeding from the cuts caused by the sharp edges of the broken crust.

We walked across the field to where the doe was lying, panting from exhaustion, in a pocket of snow. Uncle Richard slowly approached the doe, all the while talking to her very softly. He gently petted her and then put her head in his lap as he knelt in the snow, still talking in a soothing voice. We were dispatched to the barn to get the toboggan and burlap bags. We put the doe on the toboggan and pulled as Uncle Richard walked along next to the deer petting and talking to her. We brought her into the barn floor and lifted her off the toboggan. Uncle Richard said to leave the doors open about two feet so the doe could leave when she got her strength back.

That crazy deer stayed around for a week, coming and going in and out of the barn at will. Then one day she went out but did not come back. We were saddened, but Uncle Richard explained the she was a wild animal and should be free.

Weeks moved into months, and the memory of the pretty doe faded with the passing of time. Then one day in late spring we were out weeding in the garden on the hillside next to the pasture when I heard Uncle Richard say, "Gorry. Look at that!" A doe with a little spotted fawn came up out of the pasture and slowly walked up to Uncle Richard. With her tail flicking back and forth, she nuzzled him as the little fawn stood by her side. Then they both slowly trotted off. We might not understand deer talk, but it was plain to see she was saying thank you to Uncle Richard.

Uncle Richard Flagg.
This picture captures him.

Uncle Richard, leaning on the counter of the original Moody's Diner when it was a lunch stand on the Old Route 1.

Uncle Richard, his wife, Arletta, and Bertha Moody, in front of the
Moody's Cabins office in the early 1930s. Arletta was Mom's youngest sister.

With Uncle Richard around, you
knew everything would be okay.

The Flagg family, not yet complete, with four
of their eventual six children.

"Moody's Diner is more than just a good place to eat. It's a genuine Maine legend. A meal at Moody's (if you can get a seat—they're wicked busy!) is like a trip back in time to the Maine of my boyhood. The worn countertop, the waitress who has been there since forever and can reel off 37 kinds of homemade pie from memory, the pie itself, and the genuine, right-out-of-central-casting local characters sitting at the counter all add up to a 'real Maine' dining experience that simply cannot be duplicated elsewhere in the Pine Tree State."
—Tim Sample, Maine humorist and CBS News senior correspondent

Moody People

Our customers come in all shapes, colors and sizes, and from all corners of the world. We aim to serve all with good value and cheer. Many return the favor by coming back time after time. Some even drop us a line, send us photos, nominate us for recognition. We appreciate being in your thoughts. What follows is a small sampling of what you sent us over the years.

Dear Moody's,

I first visited Maine, alone, in Sept 1983. The beauty and hospitality were wonderful. The only down thing was not having someone to hear or respond when I breathed, "How beautiful!" I've been back many times, with companions, and Maine only gets better.

Last month was my first winter visit—mountains of snow on each side of the road. We loved it. One snowflake here in Georgia and everyone goes nuts, thinking that snowflake will eat the town.

Discovering Moody's Diner was the highlight of a recent visit with my son who lives in Portland. How I enjoyed your cookbook, *What's Cooking at Moody's Diner*. I read it like a novel and feel I know you. The "Best Ever Banana Bread" IS! Thank you for being there and for all that you do.

> Sincerely,
> Ann W. True
> Georgia

Ann sent us two of her own recipes—one for Earthquake Cake with this note attached: "This cake was my brother's favorite dessert until he ate your Coconut Cream Pie!"

Ann wasn't the only one taken with our Banana Bread recipe:

Dear Nancy,

I pulled out my wife's good stationary, even washed off the kitchen table to write you this letter.

About a year ago, my sister Kara bought a copy (signed by you) of *What's Cooking at Moody's Diner*. I read it cover to cover and enjoyed hearing about the colorful history of this fine diner.

Tonight my wife, Marilyn, made her first dish from your cookbook—Best Ever Banana Bread—which should have been named, Drop-Dead

Banana Bread. It was Drop Dead good!! I have never had such good coffee cake. Our four children, Laura—10, Lisa—6, Linda—4 and Michael—2, ate the rest. Laura wants to take some in her lunch tomorrow to school. I also think it came out great because Marilyn didn't burn the bottom this time, but let's credit the recipe because that's why I am writing.

The Moodys in my family all came from Laurel, Mississippi. My father was Dan Moody and his Father was John O. Moody. I am Jack Moody. (Linda and Michael helped me write this. I had to get Linda 2 cookies and take Mike to potty, all while I was trying to write you this serious thank you note with my best fountain pen.)

Anyway, my wife and I are knee-deep in raising our children, and we got discussible enjoyment out of the coffee cake recipe from your book and just wanted to write and say thanks. (We all agreed on that—first time we all agreed on something all week.)

Keep the soups hot!

> Your friend,
> Jack E. Moody
> Illinois

Dear Nancy,

This summer we started our vacation in Vermont and detoured to Waldoboro. We were not sorry. The fried clams were the best I had tasted in years—and I grew up on the end of Long Island, New York. The honey-dipped chicken was delightful and the Walnut Pie was so delicious—we hope to be back next September.

> Jane McDonough
> New York and Florida

Dear Moody's,

Your Walnut Pie is the best I've ever eaten. I've been to many parts of the world, yours is the best. Now comes the hard part—do you think I might please have the recipe?

> Betsy Baker
> Massachusetts

Betsy Baker and Jane McDonough weren't alone in their enthusiasm for our Walnut Pie.

Gourmet

October 30, 1987

Dear Chef de Cuisine:

We have received an enthusiastic letter from one of our readers about the fine food you serve in your restaurant. Our correspondent particularly admired the Walnut Cream Pie.

We wonder if you would be so gracious as to share the recipe with us. If you would like to do so, and if at some time your recipe is chosen for publication in GOURMET MAGAZINE, we will credit your restaurant and send you a complimentary copy of the issue in which the recipe appears. The decision whether or not to publish a recipe is based upon editorial needs each month.

Thank you for your time and consideration.

Sincerely yours,

Ladd Boris
Editorial Assistant

A CONDÉ NAST PUBLICATION
560 LEXINGTON AVENUE•NEW YORK, NY 10022•(212) 371-1330

The final word on our Walnut Pie comes from Marty Layne, in a review published in This Month in Maine Literature, *following the publication of the first edition of our cookbook:* "Moody's Walnut Pie, a seriously delicious concoction, threatens to drive traditional pecan pie to extinction."

Our Blueberry Muffins were honored by The Pointe Resort, Tapaito Cliffs, Arizona.

The press, local and from away, have, through the years, been kind in their coverage of the diner. Here is a sampling:

> "Moody's gets continual attention and deserves every bit of it. . . . The smell of cooked fruit and buttery pastry makes me want to eat everything in the place."
> —Kathy Grant, *Maine Times*

> "Moody's Diner is a living part of America's past, very much alive and healthy."
> —Robert Keene, *Southampton Press*, Long Island, N.Y.

Also from Long Island:

> "Moody's delivers."   —Sylvia Carter, *Newsday*

> "Nowhere else has good food and resistance to modernization made a happier combination."
> —Dave Silverbrand, *Maine Motorist* magazine

> "I love the Moody's book, because I love Moody's Diner."
> —Cynthia Hacinli, *Down East* magazine

In 1992, Moody's became a musical. Medomak Valley High School theater productions are so well regarded that their performances are always standing-room only affairs. With *Moody Blue: The Musical*, they put their reputation on the line by staging an original production in which Waldoboro's cultural and social center (Moody's Diner) was about to be replaced by an 80,000-square-foot shopping mall (by developers from away, don'cha know).

We were flattered by the excellence of the Medomak Valley Players' production, which was staged months after Dad passed away. Not many people knew, but Dad loved to sing and perform. He participated in all the plays at Lincoln Academy from his freshman year on, and in his twenties he was a member of a community theater group. Had he attended *Moody Blue: The Musical*, he would have been a toe-tapping member of the audience and very humbled that the "old hash house," as he called it, attracted so much attention.

Moody's vs. mall makings of musical

By Bruce Kyle
Of the NEWS Staff

WALDOBORO — Already pretty near eternal, Moody's Diner is about to become immortal in an original musical being cooked up at Medomak Valley High School.

"Moody Blue — The Musical," opening Nov. 5, is an expanded, song-filled adaptation of a one-act play performed by the school's fabled theater program in 1988. The new version features a script by Richard Bailey and original music by Aaron Robinson, both former students.

The 1988 play focused on Linda, a local girl who drops out of school with dreams of making it big in Boston. Fifteen years later she finds herself still waiting tables at Moody's.

In the musical, Linda is at Moody's yet, pondering her dead-end life and her on-and-off relationship with Dave Moody, owner and cook. The boredom turns to bed-

CAST MEMBERS (from left) Sam Morris, Jenn Wotton, Adam Klein and Erik Davidson share a cup

graphers, painters, poets and the just plain hungry, is here to stay.

"The talk, the rumors, going around town are a lot like the reactions of the different characters in the play," said Rick Ash, director and theater instructor. "Some are shocked, dismayed, some are elated about a mall coming to town."

Without spilling too many dramatic beans, Ash divulges that the

for kids to gather and soul of Wald makes you stop an place tradition ha

Despite having phone calls on th Ash said, "the M been very suppor contributed their o ister and counter set."

Medomak's hi

One-act play about Moody's Diner turns into a musical

By STEVE CARTWRIGHT
Staff Writer

WALDOBORO — Moody's Diner hasn't changed its orange-and-green neon sign, or anything else besides prices, in 50 years.

And in a sense, the venerable diner mirrors small-town life itself — a familiar, comfortable place to pass the time, where nothing changes.

Along with tourists and truckers, local people crack jokes and complain about the weather. And have another cup of coffee.

Moody's is the social hub of the community, and it's fame extends well beyond Waldoboro. Over the years, Moody's has spawned post cards, news stories, a Tim Sample comedy routine and a cookbook.

Never before has it inspired a musical.

Enter two local men, fresh out of Medomak Valley High School. They have teamed up with their former drama coach to create Moody Blue, a two-act musical which takes a spirited look at how small-town life revolves around a diner — and what would happen if this local institution wasn't there.

Aaron Robinson, a 1989 graduate of Medomak, is the musical half of the collaboration, composing songs such as "Waitress, Waitress." A self-taught pianist, he will play his own compositions and Gershwin's Rhapsody in Blue — theme for the musical.

Co-author is budding playwright Richard Bailey, MVHS class of '92, a drama student in Boston.

The duo expanded Moody Blue from a successful one-act play they staged while students at Medomak in 1988. Bailey made the musical an independent study project during his senior year. Robinson, taking a year off from a Boston performing arts school, has taken over from there.

Their coach is MVHS drama director Rick Ash, known for recent student productions of the "Wizard of Oz," "Peter Pan," "Annie," "42nd Street" and "Anything Goes." It's sort of a mutual-admiration society. Robinson credits Ash with giving Medomak Valley a statewide reputation for drama; Ash says he has some unusually talented students to work with.

Virtually all of them have been sell-out shows.

Ash wondered aloud if any other Maine schools had done an original musical. "We're way out on a limb," he said. But he didn't sound anxious about it. He lives in Rockport, but is no stranger to Moody's Diner. "I see it as a microcosm of the community," he said.

The ostensible plot of Moody Blue is hair-raising to fans of the diner.

A press release on the musical cleverly misleads the reader into thinking Moody's is doomed. "Rumors have been circulating," it says, that "Moody's Diner is being sold to a Boston-based firm, Felco Industries, and that the family-owned 20-acre parcel will be bulldozed to make way for an 80,000 square-foot mall."

Even this writer did a double-take when he read that. It's only true on stage, where actors take a look at what would happen if this favorite local icon were replaced by a vast, impersonal mall.

Robinson said Moody Blue is really about Linda, a 37-year-old waitress who's been serving Moody's customers for 17 years. He wanted to expand his horizons. He wasn't excited at first. He wanted to write about "my home-town diner."

"Every person in Waldoboro wants to get out," he said. So does "Linda."

"I think the thing people will be suprised about is, this is not about Moody's Diner," said Robinson. He could tell you more, but doesn't want to give away any secrets.

Moody Blue may be about life itself, and how Linda decides to live it. But the setting is unquestionably Moody's, and the Moody family has lent the production original counter stools and other props.

Another, climactic scene includes a carousel — a vehicle for music and a metaphor for the message that you can keep going around in life, or get off.

A cast of 50 includes Susan Trial as Linda, which the authors insist is not a lead role. There are no true leads among the parts, which are simply first names such as Dave (Eric Mitcheltree), Ellen (Amy Snyder), Mary (Abbey Casas), Sue (Rachel Jacobson) and so on.

Moody Blue is dedicated to Percy B. Moody, founder of the diner, who died earlier this year.

Nine public performances of the musical are set Nov. 5-7 and 11-14. Evening performances are at 7:30 p.m., with matinees Nov. 7 and 14.

Reserved tickets for evening shows are $6 each, while general admission tickets are $5 for adults, $4 for students. Matinee tickets are all $4 each. Reserved tickets must be bought through the high school on Manktown Road; other tickets are for sale at Clark's Drug in Waldoboro, Reading Corner in Rockland, and Harbor Audio Video 2, Camden.

Nov. 11, any U.S. veteran with identification will be admitted free.

For ticket information, call MVHS during school hours at 832-5389.

Reprinted courtesy of Rockland
Courier-Gazette. Used with permission.

Moody Travelers

In 1989, Neila and Mark Brownstein sent us pictures of themselves standing in front of the Pyramid of Chefron in Giza, Egypt, Mark debonairly attired in a Moody's Diner T-shirt. Mark wrote that a man approached him, saying, "Excuse me, but I have to introduce myself to anyone wearing a Moody's Diner T-shirt in Egypt." No doubt the man wanted to be associated with people of the Brownsteins' obvious good taste.

We thought the photo was fun and published it in the original edition of our cookbook. Apparently lots of other folks thought it was fun too, as we started receiving vacation photos of customers clad in Moody's Dinerware all around the world. We display the photos on a corkboard in the diner and include many of them here for you to enjoy.

Iwakuni Castle, Japan

A classic mountaineer's pose
atop Africa's Mt. Kenya.

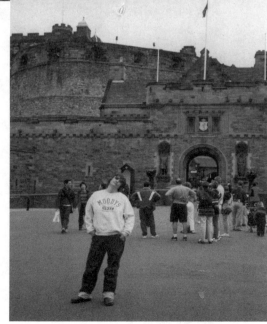

Elsewhere in Africa

Edinburgh Castle, Scotland

The Great Wall of China

The Panama Canal

Mark Brownstein at Giza, Egypt. The man and pyramid who started it all.

Dublin, Ireland

That's not only a Moody's T-shirt in Honduras, she's a Moody too—the author's granddaughter, Jasmine Olson.

The Austrian Alps

The German Alps

By the ruins in Delos, Greece

The Grand Canyon

Panmunjeon, South Korea, looking into North Korea

Machu Picchu, Peru

Alaskan Highway

Ecuador

Pointing the way from the Alaskan Highway.

A Moody Wedding

Debbie and Steve Kleinman were married June 1, 1997, (and were still married when we last checked). Their reception was unique. Debbie explains: "Imagine guests all dressed up, standing in line at a Moody's Diner buffet for franks and beans and meatloaf and mashed potatoes that were being served on trays with Moody's Diner placemats! It was definitely a day we will never forget."

Above: portrait of the new family. Below: Ready to serve some suppah.

INDEX

Apple Cake, Fresh, 139
Apple Cobbler, 50
Apple-Cranberry Raisin Pie, 135
Apple Crisp, 51
Apple Pudding, 128
Apricot-Oatmeal Muffins, 81
Baked Alaska, Grapefruit, 129
Baked Beans, Rose's, 125
Banana Bread, Best-Ever, 84
Banana Cream Pie, 59
Banana Cupcake, 58
Banana Dessert, 128
Barbecue Sauce, Lorraine's, 80

Beef Dip, Lorraine's, 64
Beet Relish, 67
Blueberry Crisp, 127
Blueberry Melt-In-Your-Mouth Cake, 139
Blueberry Muffins, 55, 81
Blueberry-Oatmeal Muffins, 82
Blueberry Pie, 60
Biscuits, Mom's, 88
Bran Muffins, 55
Bread & Butter Pickles, 65
Bread Pudding, 51, 126
BREADS, ROLLS & BISCUITS
   Banana Bread, Best-Ever, 84
   Biscuits, Mom's, 88
   Brown Bread, 84
   Cherry Peek-a- Boo Rolls, 94
   Coffee Bread, 90
   Dark Yeast Rolls, 92
   Gingerbread, 126
   Gingerbread, Mom's, 126
   Irish Freckle Bread, 91
   Johnny Cake, 47
   Nissua (Finnish Bread), 91
   Oatmeal Bread, 89
   Oatmeal Bread, Chris's, 90
   Pizza Dough, Mom's, 93
   Pizza Dough, Peg's 93
   Pumpkin Bread, Peg's, 85
   Refrigerator Rolls, 92
   Rhubarb Bread, 85
   Shredded Wheat Bread, 89
   Sixty-Minute Rolls, 93
   Strawberry, 86
   Zucchini, 86
   Zucchini-Orange, 86

Broccoli Casserole, 121
Brown Bread, 84
Brownies, 57, 154
Butter Pie, 136
"By Cracky" Bars, Aunt Bertha's, 151
Cabbage, Creamed, 121
Cabbage, Sweet and Sour Red, 121
CAKES
   Apple, Fresh, 139
   Auntie's One-Egg, 141
   Banana Cupcakes, 58
   Blueberry Melt-In-Your-Mouth, 139
   Brownies. See Cookies
   Carrot I, 140
   Carrot II, 140
   Chocolate, 143
   Chocolate Buttermilk Cupcakes, 57
   Chocolate, Crazy,144
   Chocolate, Wowie, 145
   Chocolate Torte, 131
   Coffee Cake, Blueberry Crumb, 87
   Coffee Cake, Cranberry Coffee, 87
   Coffee Cake, Prune-Apricot, 88
   Devil's Food, Filigree, 144
   Éclair Torte, 131
   Elizabeth's, 142
   Gingerbread, 126
   Gingerbread, Mom's, 126
   Hot Milk, 142
   Johnny Cake, 47
   Mocha, 143
   Oatmeal, Lazy Dazy, 146
   Peanut Butter Cupcakes, 58
   Pistachio Nut, 145
   Pound, Kaye's, 143
   Pumpkin Cake Roll, 133
   Snackin', 146
   Tomato Soup, 147
   Zucchini-Carrot, 141
CANDY
   Crunch, 166
   Fudge, Brown Sugar Peanut Butter, 165
   Fudge, Peanut Butter, 165
   Fudge, Three-Minute, 166
   Peanut Butter Balls, 165
   Reese's Squares, 166
Capesante, 108
Carrot Cake, 140
Carrots, Marinated, 122

CASSEROLES
Beef Stroganoff, Judy's, 105
Broccoli, 121
Carefree, 112
Chicken and Rice, 113
Chicken or Turkey Bake, 114
Clam, 113
Corn, Ruthie's, 113
Corn Soufflé, 122
Eggplant Parmesan, 102
Enchiladas Supreme, 111
Fish, 119
Fish, Baked, 109
Fish Fillets, Baked, 109
Ham & Potato, 114
Hearty, 114
Hungry Boys, 115
Kielbasa & Rice, 104
Macaroni and Beef, Italian, 116
Macaroni and Cheese, Mom's, 115
Mashed Potato, 118
Onions, Scalloped, w/Cheese Sauce, 124
Rice, Baked, 112
Scallop, 119
Spaghetti, 116
Spaghetti, Baked, 102
Spaghetti, Mom's, 116
Spaghetti Pie, 117
Spinach, 124
Squash, Summer, or Zucchini, 118
Tuna, Mom's, 120
Tuna Mushroom, 120
Tuna Wiggle, 120
Quickie, 119
Zucchini, 118
Zucchini, Italian, 117
Cherry Peek-a- Boo Rolls, 94
Cheese Ball I, 63
Cheese Ball II, 63
Cheese & Macaroni Salad, Marilyn's, 80
Cheeseburger Chowder, 69
Cherry Blossom Dessert, 127
Chili con Queso, 63
Chili Tostada, 105
Chocolate Buttermilk Cupcakes, 57
Chocolate Cake, 143, 144, 145
Chocolate Chip Cookies, 161
Chocolate Cream Pie, 59
Chocolate Crinkles, 152
Chocolate Doughnuts, 56, 83
Chocolate Pudding, 130
Chocolate Sauce, Mom's, 142
Chocolate Squares, Carol's, 153
Chocolate Torte, 131
Chutney Spread, 64
Clam Casserole, 113
Clam Chowder, 45
Clam Sauce, Red, 107
Clam Sauce, White, 107
Cocoa Drop Cookies, 153
Coffee Bread, 90
Coffee Cake, Blueberry Crumb, 87
Coffee Cake, Cranberry Coffee, 87
Coffee Cake, Prune-Apricot, 88
Coconut Pineapple Squares, 164
Coffee Squares, 152
COOKIES
"By Cracky" Bars, Aunt Bertha's, 151
Brownies, 57
Brownies, Chunky with Crust, 154
Brownies, Quick and Easy, 154
Chocolate Chip, 161
Chocolate Crinkles, 152
Chocolate Squares, Carol's, 153
Cocoa Drop, 153
Coconut Pineapple Squares, 164
Coffee Squares, 152
Date Balls, 157
Date Crumbles, 156
Dump Bars, 155
Gillie Whoppers, 132
Gingersnaps, 149
Hermits, Grammy Moody's, 149
Jam & Nut, 155
Molasses, Mom's Fat, 148
Molasses, Thick, 148
Oatmeal, Chewy, 150
Oatmeal, Cream-filled, 150
Oatmeal, Hermits, 149
Oatmeal Plus, 151
Old-fashioned, Filled, Mom's, 156
100 Good Cookies, 162
Peanut Butter Bars, 160
Peanut Butter, Cynthia's, 159
Peanut Butter, Double, 159
Peanut Butter Fingers, 161
Peanut, Salted, 160
Pineapple Sponge, 164
Raspberry Chews, 162
Seven-Layer Bars, 154
Shortbread, Canadian Oatmeal, 151
Sugar, 163
Sugar, Ethel's, 163
Sugar, Stir-n-Drop, 163
Corn Casserole, Ruthie's, 113

Corn Chowder, 71
Corn Soufflé, 122
Cream Filling, Basic Pie, 59
Cream Pie, Old-Fashioned, 138
Cucumber Pickles, Ripe, 66
Cucumber Relish, 67
Custard, Grape-Nut, 52
Custard Pie, 62
Dark Yeast Rolls, 92
Date Balls, 157
Date Crumbles, 156
Date Muffins, 55
DESSERTS
    Apple Cobbler, 50
    Apple Crisp, 51
    Banana Dessert, 128
    Blueberry Crisp, 127
    Cherry Blossom Dessert, 127
    Chocolate Sauce, Mom's, 142
    Grapefruit Baked Alaska, 129
    Ice-Cream, Moody's, 54
    Mincemeat, Moody's, 49
    Rhubarb Dessert, 130
    Strawberry Rhubarb Puff, 129
Devil's Food Cake, Filigree, 144
Doughnut Muffins, 83
DOUGHNUTS
    Chocolate, 56
    Chocolate, Grammy's, 83
    Molasses, Mom's, 83
    Plain, 56
DRESSINGS & SAUCES
    Barbecue Sauce, Lorraine's, 80
    Beef Dip, Lorraine's, 64
    Chocolate Sauce, Mom's, 142
    Chutney Spread, 64
    Clam Sauces, Red & White, 107
    Dressing, Lemon Garlic Salad, 79
    Spaghetti Sauce, Pesto & Basil, 101
    Sweet Sauce, Steamed Pudding, 53
    Taco Dip, 64
Éclair Torte, 131
Eggplant Parmesan, 102
Enchiladas Supreme, 111
Fajitas, 111
FISH & SEAFOOD
    Capesante, 108
    Clam Casserole, 113
    Clam Chowder, 45
    Clam Sauce, Red, 107
    Clam Sauce, White, 107
    Fish, Baked, 109
    Fish Casserole, 119
    Fish Chowder, Moody's, 45
    Fish Fillets, Baked, 109
    Haddock Fish Chowder, 74
    Lobster Bake, Mock, 109
    Salmon Loaf, Dottie's, 109
    Scallop Casserole, 119
    Shrimp Dish, Mom's Favorite, 108
    Tuna Casserole, Mom's, 120
Four-Berry Pie, 60
Freezer Pickles, 66
Fruit Salad, 75
Fudge, 165, 166
Gingerbread, 126
Gingerbread, Mom's, 126
Gingersnaps, 149
Granola Bran Muffins, 82
Granola, Easy, 167
Grapefruit Baked Alaska, 129
Grape-Nut Pudding, 52
Grape-Nut Custard Pudding, 52
Greek Pasta Salad, 79
Green Bean, Company, 122
Gumbo, Chicken, 96
Haddock Fish Chowder, 74
Ham & Potato Casserole, 114
Hamburger Soup, 70
Hash, Red Flannel, 47
Hearty Casserole, 114
Hermits, Grammy Moody's, 149
Hot Dog Relish, 67
Hot Milk Cake, 142
Hungry Boys Casserole , 115
Ice-Cream, Moody's, 54
Indian Pudding, 52, 127
Irish Freckle Bread, 91
Jam & Nut Cookies, 155
Johnny Cake, 47
Kielbasa and Rice Casserole, 104
Lasagna, American, 99
Lasagna, Crockpot, Mock, 100
Lasagna, Vegetable, 100
Lemon Chicken, 96
Lemon Garlic Dressing, 79
Lemon-Ginger Chicken Salad, 78
Lemon Meringue Pie, 61
Lemon Sponge Pie, 137
Lentil Sausage Stew, Hearty, 70
Lobster Bake, Mock, 109
Lupiers, 110
Macaroni and Beef Casserole, Italian, 116
Macaroni and Cheese, Mom's, 115
Mashed Potato Casserole, 118
Meatball Sauce, Sweet & Sour, 103

Meatballs, Loggers', 102
Meatloaf, 48, 106, 107
MEATS
    Beef Stew, Margaret's, 73
    Beef Stroganoff, Judy's, 105
    Beef or Venison Stew, Oven, 104
    Cheeseburger Chowder, 69
    Chili con Queso, 63
    Chili Tostada, 105
    Fajitas, 111
    Ham & Potato Casserole, 114
    Hamburger Soup, 70
    Hash, Red Flannel, 47
    Hearty Casserole, 114
    Hungry Boys Casserole, 115
    Kielbasa and Rice Casserole, 104
    Lasagna, Crock Pot Mock, 100
    Lasagna, American, 99
    Lentil Sausage Stew, Hearty, 70
    Lupiers, 110
    Macaroni and Beef Casserole,
        Italian, 116
    Meatloaf, Kaye's, 107
    Meatloaf, Moody's Original, 48
    Meatloaf, Moody's New, 48
    Meatloaf Roll, 107
    Meatloaf, The Best, 106
    Meatball Sauce, Sweet & Sour, 103
    Meatballs, Loggers', 102
    New England Boiled Dinner, 47
    Pork Chops & Sauerkraut, Baked, 106
    Pot Roast, Oven, 105
    Red Flannel Hash, 47
    Ribs, Braised Short, 103
    Sausage Tortellini Soup, 72
    Steakburgers, 106
    Subgum, 110
    Vegetable Beef Stew, 46
Meringue, 61, 134
Mincemeat, Moody's, 49
Minestrone Vegetable Soup, 72
Mocha Cake, 143
Molasses Bran Muffins, 82
Molasses Cookies, 148
Molasses Doughnuts, Mom's, 83
MUFFINS
    Apricot-Oatmeal, 81
    Blueberry, 81
    Blueberry, Moody's, 55
    Blueberry-Oatmeal, 82
    Bran, 55
    Date, 55
    Doughnut, 83

    Granola Bran, 82
    Molasses Bran, 82
    Pineapple, 56
Mulligatawny Soup, Marge's, 73
New England Boiled Dinner, 47
Nissua (Finnish Bread), 91
Oatmeal Bread, 89
Oatmeal Bread, Chris's, 90
Oatmeal Cake, Lazy Dazy, 146
Oatmeal Cookies, 149, 150, 151
One-Egg Cake, Auntie's, 141
Onions, Scalloped w/Cheese Sauce, 124
Orange-Pineapple Surprise Salad, 76
Party Mix, Mom's, 167
Peanut Butter Balls, 165
Peanut Butter Cookies, 159, 160, 161
Peanut Butter Cupcakes, 58
Peanut Butter Fudge, 165
Peanut Butter Pie, 137
Peanut Butter Cream Pie, 59
Peanut Cookies, Salted, 160
Pea Salad, 123
Pea Soup, 47, 74
Pecan Pies, Little, 137
PICKLES & RELISH
    Beet Relish, 67
    Bread & Butter Pickles I, 65
    Bread & Butter Pickles II, 65
    Chutney Spread, 64
    Cucumber Relish, 67
    Freezer Pickles, 66
    Hot Dog Relish, 67
    Ripe Cucumber Pickles, 66
    Zucchini Relish, 68
PIES
    Apple-Cranberry Raisin, 135
    Banana Cream, 59
    Blueberry, 60
    Butter, 136
    Chocolate Cream, 59
    Cream Filling, Basic, 59
    Cream, Old-Fashioned, 138
    Custard, 62
    Four-Berry, 60
    Lemon Meringue, 61
    Lemon Sponge, 137
    Meringue, 134
    Meringue, Never Fail, 61
    Mincemeat, Moody's, 49
    Peanut Butter, 137
    Peanut Butter Cream, 59
    Pecan, Little, 137
    Pie Crust Mom's, 134

Pie Crust No-Fail, 134
Pumpkin I, 136
Pumpkin II, 136
Refrigerator Pie, 132
Rhubarb, Fresh, 135
Rhubarb-Orange Cream, 135
Strawberry, Fresh, 61
Strawberry Rhubarb, 60
Walnut, 62
Pineapple Muffins, 56
Pineapple Sponge Cookies, 164
Pistachio Nut Cake, 145
Pizza Dough(s), 93
Pizza Rolls, 101
Pork Chops, Baked & Sauerkraut, 106
Pot Roast, Oven, 105
Potato Cheese Soup, 71
Potato Pie, 123
Potatoes, Oven-Fried, 123
Potato Salad, 77, 78
Potatoes, Twice-Baked, 124
POULTRY
    Chicken and Mushroom in Orange
        Sauce, 96
    Chicken and Rice Casserole, 113
    Chicken Divan, 95
    Chicken Divan, Curried, 95
    Chicken Gumbo, 96
    Chicken, Lemon, 96
    Chicken, Sticky, 97
    Chicken, Quick Stir-Fried, 97
    Chicken Salad, Lemon-Ginger, 78
    Chicken, Sweet & Sour, 98
    Chicken Supper, Quick 98
    Chicken or Turkey Bake, 114
    Turkey & Broccoli Quiche, 99
    Turkey Loaf, Ground, 99
Pound Cake, Kaye's, 143
PUDDINGS
    Apple, 128
    Bread, 51, 126
    Chocolate, Eggless, 130
    Chocolate, Mom's, 130
    Grape-Nut, 52
    Grape-Nut Custard, 52
    Indian, 52, 127
    Steamed w/Sweet Sauce, 53
    Tapioca, 53
Pumpkin Bread, Peg's, 85
Pumpkin Cake Roll, 133
Pumpkin Pies I & II, 136
Raspberry Chews, 162
Red Flannel Hash, 47

Refrigerator Rolls, 92
Reese's Squares, 166
Rhubarb Bread, 85
Rhubarb Dessert, 130
Rhubarb Pie, Fresh, 135
Rhubarb-Orange Cream Pie, 135
Ribs, Braised Short, 103
Rice Casserole, Baked, 112
SALADS
    Aunt Bertha's, 75
    Cheese & Macaroni, Marilyn's, 80
    Dressing, Lemon Garlic, 79
    Fruit, 75
    Greek Pasta, 79
    Green Molded, 77
    Lemon-Ginger Chicken, 78
    Martian, 76
    Mexican Taco, 79
    Mom's May Day, 77
    Orange-Pineapple Surprise, 76
    Pea, 123
    Potato, 78
    Potato, Grammie Buck's, 78
    Roberta's Sinful, 77
    Strawberry, 75
    Strawberry Pretzel, 76
    Three-Bean, 49
Salmon Loaf, Dottie's, 109
Sausage Tortellini Soup, 72
Scallop Casserole, 119
Shortbread, Canadian Oatmeal, 151
Shredded Wheat Bread, 89
Shrimp Dish, Mom's Favorite, 108
Sixty-Minute Rolls, 93
SOUPS & CHOWDERS
    Bubbling Squeak, 69
    Cheeseburger Chowder, 69
    Clam Chowder, 45
    Corn Chowder, 71
    Fish Chowder, Moody's, 45
    Haddock Fish Chowder, 74
    Hamburger Soup, 70
    Minestrone Vegetable, 72
    Mulligatawny, Marge's, 73
    Pea, 47
    Pea, Newfoundland Style, 74
    Potato Cheese, 71
    Sausage Tortellini, 72
    Taco, 71
    Tuna & Broccoli, 74
    Turkey Rice, 49
    Vegetable, 48
Spaghetti, Baked, 102

Spaghetti Casserole, 116
Spaghetti Casserole, Mom's, 116
Spaghetti Pie, 117
Spaghetti Sauce, Pesto & Basil, 101
Spinach Casserole, 124
Squash or Zucchini Casserole, 118
Steakburgers, 106
Steamed Pudding w/Sweet Sauce, 53
Stew, Margaret's Beef, 73
Stew, Hearty Lentil Sausage, 70
Stew, Oven Beef or Venison, 104
Stew, Vegetable Beef, 46
Strawberry Bread, 86
Strawberry, Pie, 61
Strawberry Rhubarb Pie, 60
Strawberry Rhubarb Puff, 129
Strawberry Salad, 75
Strawberry Pretzel Salad, 76
Subgum, 110
Sugar Cookies, 162, 163
Taco Dip, 64
Taco Salad, Mexican, 79
Taco Soup, 71

Tapioca Pudding, 53
Three-Bean Salad, 49
Tomato Soup Cake, 147
Tuna & Broccoli Soup, 74
Tuna Casserole, Mom's, 120
Tuna Mushroom Casserole, 120
Tuna Wiggle, 120
Turkey & Broccoli Quiche, 99
Turkey Loaf, Ground, 99
Turkey Rice Soup, 49
Vegetable Soup, 48
Walnut Pie, 62
WHOOPIE PIES & FILLINGS
     Cathy's, 157
     Molasses, 158
     Pumpkin, Grammie Hill's, 158
     Whoopie Pies, 58, 157
Zucchini Bread, 86
Zucchini Casserole, 118
Zucchini Casserole, Italian, 117
Zucchini-Carrot Cake, 141
Zucchini-Orange Bread, 86
Zucchini Relish, 68

Bertha and PB Moody

Thanks for stopping by.